P9-DWT-842

The
Parents
Book of Lists
FROM BIRTH TO AGE THREE

Everything You Need to Know, Do, and Buy to Keep Your Child Happy, Healthy, and Safe

By the Editors of Parents Magazine

with Marge Kennedy

Foreword by Sally Lee, Editor-in-Chief

Illustrated by Penny Carter

St. Martin's Griffin ♒ New York

The Parents

Book of Lists

FROM BIRTH TO AGE THREE

ParentsCAN

ParentsCAN
3299 Claremont Way, Ste.3
Napa, CA 94558

A Roundtable Press Book

For Roundtable Press, Inc.:

Directors: Julie Merberg, Marsha Melnick,
Susan E. Meyer

Editor: Meredith Wolf Schizer

Design: pink design, inc., nyc

Medical Advisory Board: Vicky Papadeus, M.D.;
Andrea Berne, P.C.N.P.

For Parents Magazine:

Editor in Chief: Sally Lee

Managing Editor: Mary Mohler

G+J Director of Books and Licensing: Tammy Palazzo

Library of Congress Cataloging-in-Publication Data

The parents book of lists : from birth to age three :
everything you need to know, do, and buy to keep your
child happy, healthy, and safe / by the editors of Parents
magazine with Marge Kennedy ; foreword by Sally Lee,
editor in chief ; illustrated by Penny Carter.
    p.   cm.
  ISBN 0-312-26373-2
  1. Child rearing. 2. Child development.
I. Kennedy, Marge M., 1950– II. Parents magazine
(New York, N.Y. : 1985)
HQ769.P2727 2000
649'.1—dc21   00-040252

First St. Martin's Griffin Edition: September 2000

10 9 8 7 6 5 4 3 2 1

foreword

One of the things I love about working for *Parents* magazine is that I'm exposed to information about parenting all the time. When the things you learn are constantly reinforced, they become part of your arsenal of tips, tricks, and strategies to help you deal with the many demands of parenting. And that in turn builds your confidence. So we came up with a handy, nothing-but-the-facts reference book that can be used as a refresher course in what you already know, or to fill in those little knowledge gaps we all have.

I wish I'd had this book when my daughter, Gracie, was born and I fretted that I might not be able to deal with all the situations that came up in any given day. From safety to sleep routines, from birthday bashes to the best books to read aloud, from teething to travel tips, this book provides you with all the essential information about parenting in one easy-to-use book. Best of all for busy parents, this isn't the kind of book you have to read cover to cover—just dive in and get what you need to deal with the moment at hand, whether that's a scraped knee or the rainy day blues.

Sally Lee
EDITOR-IN-CHIEF

contents

health and safety

ways to keep your baby healthy • choosing a health care practitioner • when to call 911 or your doctor for your newborn • emergencies in your baby at two months to three years • when to call the doctor for the first three years • symptoms to monitor during the first three years • your baby's checkups • how to prepare for visits to the doctor • ways to make doctor visits easier on your toddler • how to soothe a colicky baby • cold comfort • how to handle a fever • getting the temperature right • easing teething discomfort • tummy troubles • how to treat an earache • signs of hearing impairment • who's at risk for hearing loss? • symptoms of visual impairment • motor development: looking for signs of delay • first-aid kit essentials

household safety tips • bedroom basics • crib safety checklist • things to know about your child's bedding • changing table rules • playpen safety • kitchen hazards • make your eating area safer • high-chair pointers • bathroom safety checks • laundry room checks • steps to stair safety • common furniture hazards • heating and air conditioning systems • make electrical appliances safe • fire safety rules • backyard safety • how to make your outdoor pool safer

chapter 2   77

everyday routines

chapter 5 175

special events

chapter 6

relationships

introduction

*t*he *Parents Book of Lists* is designed for parents like you—smart, caring, and busy—who want advice quickly and in an easy-to-find format. *The Book of Lists* is organized into six sections: Health and Safety includes the information you need on obtaining the right medical care, childproofing, and teaching healthy habits to your child. Everyday Routines helps you plan your child's day, from eating a nutritious breakfast to getting a good night's rest. Playtime Fun and Learning is chock-full of ideas to enhance your child's intellectual and emotional growth. Travel and Everyday Outings offers a road map to family safety and comfort while away from home. Special Events helps you plan and celebrate momentous occasions as well as deal with life's inevitable difficulties. And, finally, the Relationships section offers strategies for making meaningful connections within the family and between your family and your community.

Though created primarily as a quick-reference source, *The Parents Book of Lists* will also prove useful as an overview of the child-development and child-safety issues that matter most to you during your child's early years, helping you avoid problems before they occur and making the most of your time with your baby and toddler.

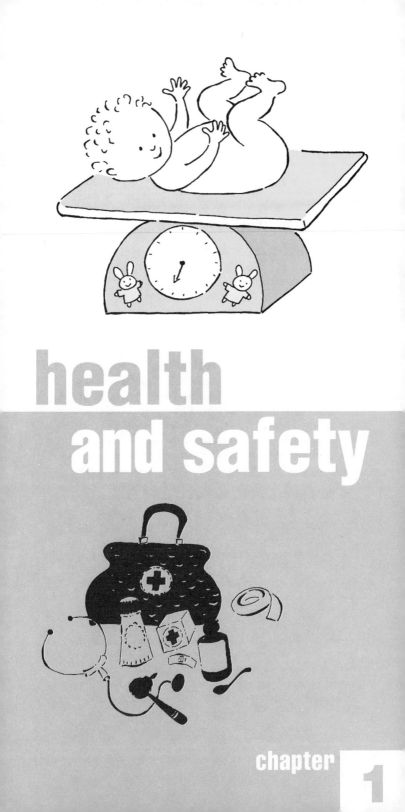

health
and safety

medical care

because a baby's immune system isn't fully functional, you'll want to take extra care to ensure that she's
not unnecessarily exposed to germs and allergens, especially during infancy. To keep your baby healthy:

1 breast-feed, if possible Numerous studies have
shown that breast-feeding during the first year reduces
the incidence of asthma, ear infections, and colds in
babies and that the protection offered in these early
months can last many years. However, if you cannot
nurse, don't make yourself crazy with guilt (or allow
anyone else to).

2 avoid smoke and exhaust fumes Keep your
baby away from cigarette and cigar smoke, as well as
smoke from fireplaces and wood stoves. Avoid traffic
congestion, and stay downwind at barbecues. Kids
who are exposed to smoke and other toxins are more
likely to develop ear infections, allergies, and breathing problems. Be sure that you have a working smoke
detector and carbon monoxide detector in your home.

3 keep your home lead-free Check the water,
paint, and dust in your home and the soil outside for
lead using a store-bought kit, or hire a professional.
To find a lead inspector in your area, call 800-424-
LEAD or go to *www.leadlist.com*. Also, if you live
in a heavily trafficked area, wipe down windowsills
and wet-mop the floors beneath open windows.

4 avoid germ-ridden environments If at all possible, hold off on visits to the mall, treks on the subway,
or airline flights, all of which offer too much exposure
to germs during your baby's first six weeks. This type
of travel is tough on new mothers as well. If you can't
avoid these environments, it's best to hold your baby
in a front carrier facing your chest. If at all possible,
don't enroll your child in day care for the first six
months of her life, since day-care centers cannot rea-

sonably keep other children—even those with runny noses—at a safe distance from your baby. If a family member or houseguest has a cold, he or she should avoid breathing directly on your baby. Limit the number of people handling newborns.

5 wash your hands thoroughly Wash with warm water and soap before handling your baby. Insist that anyone handling your baby (especially during the first three months) wash well first.

6 watch your diet If there's a strong history of allergies in your family, avoid peanuts, shellfish, and anything else you have an allergy to while you're nursing. These are most likely to affect your child if she's exposed to them during her first year. It's also best to avoid any foods that give you stomach troubles.

choosing a health care practitioner

f or the first few years of your child's life, you'll rely on no one—not even your partner or your mother—as much as you do your baby's pediatrician or nurse practitioner. Ask your obstetrician or friends in your neighborhood for recommendations, and be sure to ask the right questions as you begin your search to help you find the right match. In addition to finding out about which insurance plan a doctor takes, you'll want to ask:

1 what are your credentials? Your best bet is a pediatrician or family practitioner with considerable training in the care of children. Make sure she is board-certified in pediatrics or family medicine, as well as licensed by your state in her area of specialty. (For information about a doctor's certification, call the American Board of Medical Specialists at 800-733-2267. For information about a nurse practitioner's certification, call the New York State Board of Nursing at 518-474-3845. Also look at the office walls, where degrees should be prominently displayed.)

2 what is your hospital affiliation? You'll want a doctor who's affiliated with a good hospital. Note that the best hospital for pediatrics might not be the one that's closest to your home.

3 how do I reach you after hours? Your doctor must be willing and able to discuss your concerns even if they occur at two in the morning. Her manner should never make you feel foolish for your worries, but should reassure you that your calling—at any time—is the right thing to do when you have questions about your baby's health.

4 who covers for you when you're not available? Physicians in small or large group practices have built-in backups if the doctor cannot see you. You'll probably want to meet at least some of them before signing on with any group. If the doctor is working independently, who covers for her? Be sure that physician is located conveniently, and treats referrals with the same care as he or she does regular patients.

5 do you advise breast-feeding or circumcision? You'll want to be sure that your doctor's philosophy is in line with your own.

6 how do you handle reducing a patient's pain? The doctor's attitude toward pain medication and the use of antibiotics should be thoughtful and clearly explained to you.

7 are you willing to discuss immunizations? Your health care provider ought to be willing to answer your questions, discuss the schedule of immunizations, and patiently address any concerns you may have.

8 do you discuss nonmedical issues? Many pediatricians take the time to talk about your child's behavior and routines, and other family issues, in great depth.

9 what's the average waiting-room time? Ask at what intervals appointments are scheduled. Check out the office ambience and supplies—are there toys and books to keep kids entertained while they wait?

when to call 911 or your doctor for your newborn

during your baby's first two months of life, all medical issues are important, and pediatricians expect to hear from you often. Throughout the first eight weeks, if anything concerns you, you shouldn't hesitate to call the doctor. Call your doctor and/or 911 immediately if:

1 something scares you Parents are very perceptive. If your newborn looks or behaves in a way that makes you feel that something is seriously wrong—his coloring looks off, he is limp and lethargic, or just looks sick to you—even if you can't articulate your fear or concern, call the doctor.

and call immediately if your newborn experiences:

2 fever In the first two months, if your child has a temperature of 100.4 degrees F or higher taken rectally, call your doctor right away.

3 breathing problems If your child appears to be struggling to breathe, is pale, or has difficulty catching his breath, seek help immediately.

4 an accident or trauma If the baby falls, or is in an accident that may have caused a head injury or fracture or any other trauma, he should be examined even if he appears to be unhurt. Also seek help if he's burned, or if there's bleeding. If your newborn loses consciousness, call 911 right away. It's usually best not to try to transport an injured infant yourself, since handling could cause additional damage, so call first for advice.

5 seizure Call for emergency assistance if your baby's arms and legs are flailing uncontrollably, his head falls back, and his eyes roll back into his head.

6 decreased feeding If there's a significant reduction in urine or stool, and your newborn is feeding noticably less, notify your doctor right away.

7 excessive crying Newborns usually cry when they're hungry or simply want to be held. If your baby's crying is incessant and is not soothed with cuddling or feeding, call the doctor to determine if something's wrong.

8 change in the fontanel A depression in your baby's "soft spot" on the top of his head could indicate dehydration and should be attended to right away.

emergencies in your baby at two months to three years

Your baby's immune system matures every day, and by eight weeks she is infinitely sturdier than when she was first born. So while not every anomaly is cause for concern, the following conditions do warrant an immediate call to your pediatrician and/or 911.

1 a toxic look If your child appears limp and unresponsive, or simply looks scary to you, it's important to call the doctor right away.

2 breathing difficulty As with newborns, if your child appears to be struggling to breathe, is pale, or has difficulty catching her breath, it is a medical emergency.

3 seizure Call for emergency assistance if your baby's arms and legs are flailing uncontrollably, her head falls back, and her eyes roll back into her head.

4 accidents or trauma If your child loses consciousness or suffers a head injury or burn; if you suspect a fracture; or if there's excessive bleeding or an injury to the eyes or teeth, seek medical help immediately.

5 ingestion Be especially wary if your child has swallowed iron supplements; any type of medicine (including an overdose of infant or children's medicine); herbal remedies; spices, plants, or other substances you're not sure about. Call your doctor and/or 911 as well as calling poison control. Keep your local poison control number posted in a prominent place.

6 allergic reactions If your child experiences difficulty breathing or swallowing, or develops hives as a result of an insect sting, seasonal allergies, or something she has eaten, alert your doctor right away.

7 reactions to vaccines If your child has a fever over 102 degrees F; seems extremely lethargic or unresponsive within 48 hours of a vaccine, report these symptoms to your doctor immediately.

8 choking It's common for children to gag, especially when they're teething or first learning to eat. However, if your child is changing color or unable to vocalize, it's an emergency.

parents ALERT!

handling blood Wear non-latex gloves when cleaning up blood spills (if anyone in the home cuts himself and leaves a small puddle on clothing, furniture, or the floor). And clean the bloodied surface with a bleach solution. All blood, no matter whose it is, should be handled as something that could carry infection.

when to call the doctor for the first three years

If you're ever really worried about your child's health, do not hesitate to call your pediatrician at any time of day or night. It's always important to be attentive to changes in your child's appearance and behavior, but be assured that if he seems generally healthy and normal, there is probably no cause for alarm. Depending on your child's age and the severity of the signs, symptoms, and behaviors, you can probably wait until regular hours to call your doctor about the following, but do call if you notice:

1 changes in behavior In a nonverbal child, a glassy-eyed, sick look; a lack of responsiveness; excessive sleepiness or wakefulness; continuous or high-pitched crying all indicate that something is wrong.

2 pain A verbal child can tell you when something hurts. If your baby is in pain, he will likely be irritable and difficult to console, and will have a hard time feeding. Babies with ear infections are uncomfortable lying down and may start shrieking when placed in a horizontal position.

3 rapid, uncomfortable breathing If you see your child's ribs, stomach or neck muscles working; hear him wheezing; or if he has a persistent cough that's disrupting his sleep, bring him in to see the doctor.

4 limpness If your baby seems limp or isn't using his arms or legs, or your toddler's gait seems funny, let your doctor know.

5 changes in coloration A blue tinge to your baby's face, fingernails, or toenails, or a pale, ashen appearance may indicate a breathing or circulatory problem. A yellow tinge to the skin or the white of the eyes may suggest jaundice or another liver condition.

6 prolonged fever Your child's fever is a clue that his body is fighting an infection, a healthy response. And he may be running a temperature for a day or so and be otherwise healthy and happy. However, if he doesn't respond to fever-reduction medication such as ibuprofen or acetaminophen within several doses, or if he seems uncomfortable and sick, you should check in with your doctor.

7 excessive vomiting or diarrhea Although spitting up can be forceful and therefore confused with vomiting, a child who spits up seems and is perfectly fine. When he vomits, he is and feels sick so you should call the doctor.

8 changes in urine output Report any significant increase or decrease.

9 changes in bowel movements Report a substantial change in the frequency, color, or consistency of the stool.

10 blood in urine or in the stool

11 unusual skin rashes Spots, blisters, canker sores, hives, or any red, weepy, yellow, crusted spots on your child's skin should be examined.

12 spreading skin infection Any warm, red, tender, irritated area that appears to be spreading should be seen by a doctor.

13 minor injuries that don't heal If your child hurts his finger and it's hurting (or worse) two days later, call the doctor. Also check in if he has a wound that looks red, yellow, or pussy.

14 a nosebleed that's hard to stop Call the doctor if it takes longer than ten minutes to stop the bleeding by gently pinching the nose, applying ice, and holding the head back.

15 any minor symptoms that get worse or don't resolve A cold should go away in two weeks. If, during the course of the cold your child develops a high fever or a severe cough, alert your doctor.

16 swollen eyes, hands, or feet

17 eye pain or discharge

18 progressive abdominal pain If your child has a simple tummy ache, he will writhe or wriggle and typically feel better if you rub it. However, if he does not want to be touched or moved and cannot stand (he would rather lie perfectly still), he may have appendicitis or another internal problem.

19 a distended belly Alert the doctor if your child has a bloated or tender abdomen.

20 a bulge in the crotch or by the belly button This may indicate a hernia.

21 multiple bruises on the upper body A doctor should examine any unexplained bruising in odd places.

22 scrotal swelling or pain (in boys) This may indicate a hernia or undescended testicles.

preventing choking during vomiting During any incidence of vomiting, position your child on her side or upright with her head forward to prevent her from inhaling the expelled material.

emergency rash Petechia is a rash that looks like pinpoint bleeding (bright red spots) under the skin. It may appear in conjunction with excessive vomiting or be associated with rare infections. Call your doctor immediately if your child has a rash that fits this description.

symptoms to monitor during the first three years

keep a running list of anything that strikes you as odd about your child's behavior or development. Your regular well-baby checkups are a good time to discuss these concerns. However if you're not scheduled to see the doctor for several months, call him to discuss your observations and schedule an appointment sooner. Things you should take note of include:

1 any indication of hearing or vision problems (See pages 38–40 and 41–42 for symptoms.) Also look out for funny eye movements, wandering eyes, squinting, or watery, drippy, crusty eyes.

2 any concerns about developmental delays If you feel like your child is significantly behind her peers, discuss it with your doctor. For a list of symptoms of developmental delay, see pages 42–43.

3 unusual behaviors Your pediatrician can advise you on common problems such as sleep disturbances and night terrors; nutrition or feeding techniques; and tantrums. He should also be able to help you in dealing with family changes such as a move, death, or divorce.

your baby's checkups

regular checkups are one of the best ways to ensure your child's health. Here's what you're likely to encounter.

first, the nurse will check:

1 height and weight Your baby's size will be compared to her last visit and to other babies of her sex and age.

2 head circumference Measured in centimeters, the doctor will want to confirm that your baby's head is growing normally—that it's larger than the last visit, in roughly the same percentile as the last visit, and within the normal range.

3 temperature Anything between 98.6 and 100.4 degrees F is considered normal.

the doctor's physical exam goes from head to toe:

4 head The doctor will examine size and shape and the fontanel to be sure that it's closing at an appropriate pace. (It should be closed by about 18 months.)

5 eyes Your baby's eyes should have a clear appearance and her pupils should respond correctly to light.

6 ears The doctor will also check to see that ears are free from infection and that your child is responding to sound and voice.

7 mouth and nose The doctor will look for teeth and check for cavities, as well as inspecting the throat and tonsils.

8 neck The neck should have a normal range of motion, and glands should have a normal size and shape.

9 heart and chest The doctor will be on the lookout for a murmur or other symptoms of heart irregularities and for ease of breathing, noting any wheezing or rasping, signs of allergies, or other conditions.

10 abdomen Your practitioner will feel for normal liver and spleen size, as well as checking pulses and glands.

11 rectum and genitals The rectum should have a normal opening without rashes or sores. *In boys:* the doctor will examine the testes to see that they are palpable in the scrotum; infants will be checked for proper healing of circumcision. *In girls:* the doctor checks the vaginal opening for labial fusion and discharge.

12 neurological functions Depending on your child's age, the doctor will evaluate various reflexes by tickling or pinching her foot to see if she automatically withdraws and curls her toes; tapping below the knee with a rubber hammer; and holding her upright to be sure that she's "stepping." Throughout the appointment, your pediatrician will be observing your child's motions and reflexes.

13 musculoskeletal development Your doctor will examine the spine; muscle tone and strength; and in newborns, the hips, for proper alignment. Depending on your child's age, the doctor may want to see her pull up, walk, climb, or roll over.

typically after (or possibly during) the physical exam, the doctor will talk to you about your child's history; she'll want to know about:

14 what's gone on since the last visit? You should report any illnesses, accidents, or injuries.

15 behavior and development Throughout the examination, the doctor will observe your child, noting if she's meeting general motor and language developmental milestones, such as sitting up and vocalizing at the appropriate ages. Discuss any concerns you may have.

16 your child care arrangements If relevant, talk about your child's school or child care provider, and how she has adjusted.

17 urine output and bowel habits The doctor will ask about the frequency, consistency, color, and quantity of your baby's diaper output.

18 your family environment If only one parent is present at the appointment, the doctor may ask about the other partner's involvement. She'll also want to know about siblings or any other family issues.

19 safety Once your child is mobile, your pediatrician should prompt you to childproof your home, ensuring that you have window bars, outlet covers, and other safety essentials. (See pages 47–67 for more information about childproofing.)

20 routines Your doctor will advise you on healthy eating and sleeping routines.

21 your concerns Your doctor should ask you or you should offer your own observations and questions regarding your child's physical, emotional, and intellectual development.

how to prepare for visits to the doctor

to keep early visits simple:

1 call ahead Confirm your appointment and find out if there's an unusually long wait. If so, ask if you can come in later, to allow the overflow crowd to be seen before you arrive.

2 dress your baby in easy-on/easy-off clothes Your aim is to make your baby comfortable and to fuss over clothing as little as possible.

3 carry a receiving blanket Most babies hate to be naked, especially in a doctor's chilly office.

4 make sure your child is well-fed A hungry baby is a cranky baby. Try feeding your child before arriving even if it's not his regular feeding time.

5 bring a written list of questions and concerns Also pack a notebook to write down any instructions from the doctor.

6 pack a few distractions For babies beyond the newborn stage, a comforting toy from home can greatly reduce any anxiety amid the strange sounds and smells of the office.

did you know?

Some doctors schedule regular checkups for young babies for a certain time of the week so they won't be exposed to other sick children in the waiting room. See if your doctor has this sort of scheduling policy.

ways to make doctor visits easier on your toddler

in addition to the suggestions above:

1 be flexible If you arrive at the office and find that you'll be waiting for more than 20 minutes, check in and notify the support staff that you'll be back a bit later. Be prepared to take your child for a walk or other diversion rather than confining her to the waiting room. Even if there are toys in the office, it's not a good idea for your child to play with things that may have been mouthed or handled by sick children.

2 be matter-of-fact about the visit Prepare your child by saying something like, "Today the doctor is going to see how much you've grown," to put the plans in a positive light.

3 play doctor at home A toy doctor's kit designed especially for toddlers gives them familiarity with the tools of the trade, as well as the opportunity to practice kindness and caring on their dolls.

4 let your child make something for the doctor Doing something such as drawing a picture to give to the doctor can encourage your toddler to feel a personal connection with her pediatrician. Upon receiving your child's handmade gift, the doctor will no doubt praise it, making your toddler feel happy to be there.

5 offer small rewards for cooperation

Nonmaterial rewards, such as a visit to the playground after the doctor's visit, can help encourage cooperation, as can small trinkets such as stickers and lollipops from the doctor. Avoid making lavish promises such as buying a toy in return for cooperation, since your savvy tot will soon learn to demand payment for doing what's expected of her.

6 offer patience and understanding

Especially if your child needs to have an immunization or other unpleasant procedure, be sure to be clearly on your child's side. Honestly acknowledge to your child that something may hurt and give her a concrete way to deal with it. You might say, "Hug me as tight as you can until it's over," or you might engage your child in singing her favorite song at the top of her lungs during the procedure. Or just let her know it's okay to scream and cry.

how to soothe a colicky baby

Colic is a condition that causes pain in your infant's gastrointestinal tract. Fortunately, it rarely lasts beyond your baby's third month, and usually peaks at about four to six weeks of age. Symptoms include apparent abdominal pain, gassiness, a distended belly, irritability, and long, inconsolable bouts of crying, usually starting in the early evening and lasting for hours. No one is really sure of the cause, but many physicians cite the baby's diet—either something the nursing mother is eating, or a sensitivity to formula. To soothe your child during bouts of colic:

1 walk him kangaroo-style

With your baby in a front carrier (facing either in or out, depending on what seems to be his preference) walk him around the house, or, if weather permits, outside. In cultures in which babies are regularly strapped to their moms, the incidence of colic is much lower than in the West.

2 hold him in the "colic carry"

Position your baby so that his stomach rests on your forearm and his head is supported in the palm of your hand or the crook of your arm.

3 rock and roll him Rock your baby in your arms. Take him for a ride in the car, or for a walk in his stroller. The steady rhythm of any kind of movement is soothing.

4 make good vibrations Place your child, securely strapped in his car seat, on top of a running clothes dryer, being sure to hold the seat to prevent it from vibrating off the machine.

5 swaddle him Some babies respond well to being wrapped tightly, especially while being rocked.

6 give him a massage Lay him across your legs and gently rub his back to help release pent-up gas.

7 play "white noise" A single sound, such as a recording of rain or even the sound of a hair dryer, can calm your baby.

8 reduce outside stimulation Lower the lights, reduce the noise around the house, and speak or sing softly to your baby.

9 provide warmth Place a warm (not hot) wash-cloth on his tummy or give him a warm bath.

10 pedal his legs With your baby on his back, gently move his legs in a pedaling motion to help him release gas.

11 adjust his diet If you're nursing and if none of the above seems to help, try changing your own diet by eliminating dairy products, caffeine, onions, cabbage, broccoli, garlic, and spicy foods. If your baby is formula-fed, ask the pediatrician about switching to a soy-based, predigested, or other hypoallergenic formula. Formula-fed babies need iron, so low-iron formulas are rarely recommended.

12 calm yourself If all else fails, put the baby down, make yourself a cup of tea and calm yourself down. Don't let him pick up on your own anxiety. Then snuggle your baby and realize that you're the best person to comfort him and if you can't do it, nobody can.

cold comfort

Cold symptoms, such as runny noses, congestion, and coughs, may be caused by allergies as well as by any of the more than 200 known cold viruses. Always alert the doctor if your child's symptoms are severe or worsening, or new signs and symptoms develop such as fever and severe cough. Normal colds last 7 to 14 days. In the meantime, to help your child—and you—breathe easier:

1 run a cool-mist humidifier in her room Be sure to clean the humidifier daily, according to the manufacturer's recommendations.

2 use saline drops to unstuff her nose Just a few drops in each nostril, especially before mealtime and bedtime, will soften the mucus. Be sure to use unmedicated saline drops for babies under six months of age.

3 use a bulb syringe When nose mucus is thick, a bulb syringe—best used after applying saline drops—can quickly unclog the secretions.

4 keep your child hydrated Ingesting fluids helps thin mucus, so offer extra breast or bottle feedings for infants and lots of fluids to older kids. And, yes, chicken soup does help.

5 elevate your child's head while sleeping Place a book or a rolled towel under the head of her mattress to raise her head slightly. This helps drain the nasal passages while she sleeps. Never put a pillow or other prop directly under your child's head before the age of two, since younger children can be smothered by them.

6 give your child a warm bath The warm steamy room will help her breathe easier.

7 offer a pain reliever or fever reducer If your child is in pain or has a fever, ask your pediatrician about giving her either acetaminophen (such as Tylenol) or ibuprofen (such as Motrin). It's essential that you follow the dosage recommendations carefully.

cough medicines Before choosing or using an over-the-counter cough medicine or decongestant, check with your provider, because different types of coughs require different responses. A cough caused by an infection may require an antibiotic, not a cough syrup. A cough caused by an allergy may respond to an antihistamine.

how to handle a fever

a fever is a symptom of an underlying condition, not an illness in itself. Remember: If your child is under two months of age, report any fever over 100.4 degrees F; After the age of two months, any temperature over 101.0 degrees F is considered a fever. If your child seems otherwise happy, there's probably no cause for alarm even if he is running a fever. If, however, he seems sick and uncomfortable, call your health care provider. To ease your child's discomfort from a mild fever:

1 **offer fever-reducing medication** Acetaminophen or ibuprofen can help reduce symptoms. Consult with your doctor for proper dosages if giving medication to your child under age two. Never give children of any age aspirin, because it can cause a rare but serious condition called Reye syndrome, which could damage the brain and liver.

2 **offer plenty of fluids** To reduce the risk of dehydration, offer extra breast or bottle feedings to infants and other liquids to older children.

3 **dress your child lightly** While you don't want to give your child a chill, it's important that you don't overdress him either. At home, keep him dressed in comfortable, lightweight clothing. Don't use heavy blankets in bed.

4 **give a cool bath** Make sure it's lukewarm to cool, but not so cold that he's shivering.

getting the temperature right

The most accurate way to get an infant's temperature is with a rectal thermometer, either mercury-based or digital. Digital ear thermometers vary, but are more accurate with children over age one. An infant's ear canal is too shallow to allow an accurate reading. For armpit readings, a mercury thermometer must be held in place for at least five minutes to get the most accurate reading. Forehead strips do not give accurate core-body readings. If your child has been bundled up in excess clothing or has been running around, let him cool down for 20 minutes or so before taking his temperature.

easing teething discomfort

most babies begin teething at about four to five months of age, and children continue teething throughout adolescence. While teething is a fact of life, excessive teething pain needn't be. To help your child maintain her smile while incisors and molars are making their first appearance:

1 clean up drool Irritation to the sensitive skin around your child's mouth can cause discomfort. Use a clean, damp cloth to wash away drool. Follow with a mild moisturizer to combat dryness and chapping.

2 offer pain relievers Topical ointments made for teething pain and medications such as acetaminophen and ibuprofen can be helpful.

3 keep safe teethers on hand Commercially made teethers, such as cold rings, can greatly reduce gum pain. Avoid homemade teethers such as frozen spoons, frozen bagels, and cold rags, which present choking and gagging hazards.

4 offer cold treats If your child is eating solid food, offer chilled fruit snacks or frozen yogurt.

tummy troubles

knowing the cause of upset stomach is your first step in treating it.

1 if your child is constipated Encourage lots of water drinking, or any fluids. Add high-fiber foods such as mashed or strained prunes, apricots, beans, or diluted prune juice to your child's diet. If you are nursing, you can try eating some prunes. For toddlers, add fresh fruits and vegetables. Cut back on binding foods such as rice, bananas, and apples. Encourage lots of water drinking.

2 if your child has diarrhea Offer lots of liquids every half hour or so, both sweet and salty (diluted juice and broth, for example). If your pediatrician recommends, give your child an oral rehydration therapy such as Pedialyte. Feed him binding foods such as applesauce, bananas, and rice.

parents ALERT!

avoid nonprescribed medication Medicines for gas, diarrhea, or constipation should not be given without your doctor's approval. Avoid any medications, such as Pepto Bismol, that contain aspirin, since aspirin can lead to liver disease. Avoid ibuprofen, which may cause further stomach upset. Acetaminophen, however, can be used to treat accompanying headache or fever.

how to treat an earache

earaches are among the most common of childhood illnesses. To treat an infection or ease the pain:

1 **have your child examined** Your pediatrician will be able to diagnose the cause of her pain.

2 **use antibiotics wisely** Not all ear infections should be treated with antibiotics. Overuse of antibiotics can lead to antibiotic-resistant strains of the bacteria. Under the age of two, most children do need antibiotics to treat an ear infection because they are more susceptible to spreading infection. In older children, with recurring ear infections or an earache accompanied by fever and severe pain—or if your child seems truly sick—it's best to treat with antibiotics. It's also essential to complete the course (usually ten days) of the medicine. If, however, your child is not otherwise ill, is over two, and you can come back for a follow-up visit 48 hours later, you can probably skip the antibiotics and let the infection run its course. If you opt for this route, it's important to watch your child closely.

3 **don't use over-the-counter eardrops** And never put water in your child's ear.

4 encourage your child to sit up Maintaining an upright position helps the ears drain naturally.

5 keep the ears warm A hat with ear flaps is the best protection from wind and cold outdoors. A warm compress can also reduce pain, but only if your pediatrician has assured you that there is no abscess (warmth could cause an abscess to burst).

6 encourage frequent swallowing Sucking on a popsicle, or drinking juice or water, will help open the eustachian tubes, relieving pressure.

7 offer pain relievers Children's-strength ibuprofen or acetaminophen can be helpful.

signs of hearing impairment

hearing loss can be subtle and can show up at any time, so you'll want to check your child's hearing periodically, particularly if he's had frequent ear infections or shows any signs of hearing loss. If an infant is at high risk of hearing loss (see box on page 40), he should be tested at birth. Otherwise, hearing tests are not generally given as part of routine examinations until age three, as part of the preschool well-child visit to the pediatrician. If you suspect hearing loss, have your child tested immediately, since difficulty hearing will lead to language and learning delays. What to look for:

at birth to age six months your baby:

- **does not awaken to loud noises or voices nearby** Loud noises do not startle or frighten him.
- **doesn't look to find the source of a new sound**
- **babbles, but not in response to others** Likewise, he doesn't repeat sounds such as "ahh," "ooh," and "ba-ba" by the age of six months.
- **isn't attracted to noisemaking toys like rattles**
- **isn't soothed by your voice** Or he doesn't turn

his head in the direction of your voice, or doesn't smile when you speak to him.

- **seems surprised by seeing you** He seems startled even though you've made some noise when approaching him while outside his field of vision.

at six to ten months your baby:

- **doesn't respond to everyday household noises** He should respond to such noises as the ringing telephone, a doorbell, or conversation.
- **doesn't seem to recognize oft-repeated words** He should recognize "bye-bye" and his own name.
- **doesn't babble when he plays**
- **doesn't respond to simple requests** "Look at this" or similar requests should elicit a response.
- **doesn't look at things you talk to him about**
- **doesn't become engaged in conversation** Unless he's making eye contact.

at 10 to 18 months your toddler:

- **doesn't experiment with vocalizing** For example, he should try out different sounds, or vary the pitch and volume.
- **doesn't point to familiar objects when asked** He doesn't respond to simple directions, such as "Give me the teddy bear."
- **doesn't imitate simple words and sounds**
- **doesn't enjoy word games** Most babies enjoy peek-a-boo and pat-a-cake, for example.
- **has a vocabulary of fewer than three words**

at 18 to 36 months your child:

- **doesn't respond to yes/no questions** Such as "Do you want a cookie?"
- **doesn't understand simple phrases** Such as "in the box" or "not now."
- **doesn't follow simple directions** Such as "Give me the book."

- **doesn't enjoy being read to**
- **cannot distinguish similar-sounding words**
  Such as "for" and "door."
- **doesn't respond to music by singing, dancing, or clapping**

at three to four years your child:

- **frequently tugs at one or both ears**
- **tends to favor one ear while listening** He turns his head so that his ear faces the source of the sound.
- **turns the TV or music volume too high**
- **frequently complains of ear pain** Or complains of a ringing sound in his ears.

did you know?

Exposing your infant to music can aid in his speech development, since it encourages listening skills and promotes the ability to differentiate pitches.

who's at risk for hearing loss?

abies born prematurely (under three pounds, four ounces); those who spent any time in the neonatal intensive-care unit for any abnormality, birth injury, or illness; those with craniofacial malformations such as cleft palate; children with Down syndrome; and those with a family history of hearing problems are at increased risk of hearing loss. In addition, children who have had bacterial meningitis, head injuries, frequent ear infections, exposure to certain antibiotics and other medications, or who are exposed to excessive noise, may also develop hearing problems.

symptoms of visual impairment

newborns are barely able to make out any distinct images more than 8 to 15 inches away. In addition, a very young baby is unable to distinguish colors clearly, seeing sharp contrasts, but not differences in similar tones. Her vision progresses from about 20/400, which means she can see at 20 feet what a person with perfect vision could see at 400 feet, to about 20/70 by three months of age. By six months, a baby's vision is fully formed, in both clarity and color awareness. Though infants' eyes are checked at birth and during all doctor visits, you should be on the lookout for, and alert your pediatrician if your child shows, any of the following signs of visual difficulty.

in infants:

- **any clouding of the eyes** May indicate cataracts.
- **any discharge from the eye** Discharge or crustiness around the eyelid could signal an infection.
- **excessive tearing** Tearing or mucus buildup in one or both eyes could point to a blocked tear duct.
- **inability to follow you with her eyes** She seems to have difficulty finding you as you tend to her or move around the room.
- **lack of interest** She doesn't reach out for toys or other objects by 12 weeks.

in older babies and toddlers:

- **examines things extremely close up** For instance, she puts a book right up to her nose or sits only inches from the TV, both signs of nearsightedness, or holds things at arm's length to view, a possible sign of farsightedness.
- **cocks her head to see** And she appears to be looking at most things from the corner of her eye.
- **lacks interest in toys** And she seems to ignore other visually appealing objects, as well as activities that require visual involvement, such as coloring and block building.
- **rubs eyes frequently** Or she blinks or squints excessively.

- **has frequent headaches**
- **displays poor eye-hand coordination**
- **shows apparent clumsiness** She often bumps into people and things.
- **appears to favor one eye**
- **can't recognize and name colors by age three** This may indicate color blindness, a relatively common condition, especially in boys.
- **is extremely sensitive to light**
- **eyelids droop or appear enlarged**
- **has one eye that wanders or crossed eyes**

motor development: looking for signs of delay

there's a wide range of normal development as a child moves from a squirming infant to a running toddler. While there's no need for concern if your child sits up a month later than one of his peers, it's important to talk to your child's pediatrician if your child is seriously behind these ages for reaching certain stages of motor development:

1 **lifting his head** While a newborn can lift his head a few inches for a moment or so, by two months, most babies can raise their head and shoulders when placed on their tummies.

2 **swiping at and grasping objects** Infants are born with a reflex to grasp, though their ability to do so reflexively stops at about two months. By this age, babies begin deliberate swiping at objects that interest them. The ability to grasp purposefully comes at about four to five months.

3 **rolling over** Some babies can roll themselves from their sides to their backs as early as three months of age. Most reach this milestone by four months.

4 sitting up while propped By about four months, most babies can sit up if propped on pillows, though they may topple over after a few moments.

5 sitting up unaided This milestone usually takes place between six and seven months, first with your baby balancing herself with her arms and then assuming a more upright position unaided, perhaps even holding a toy while sitting.

6 crawling Crawling usually begins at about eight to nine months of age.

7 standing while holding on About a month after learning to crawl, most babies will attempt to pull themselves up by holding on to a prop such as the sofa or a table.

8 walking There's a wide range, from 9 to 16 months, in which babies become mobile while upright. They will usually take their first steps holding on to a prop, eventually letting go and making solo steps with their feet wide apart. By 18 months, most will adopt the typical heel-to-toe gait.

9 climbing stairs By 18 months, most toddlers will climb up stairs, one foot at a time, while holding on. Many will choose to come down stairs either on their bottoms or as if climbing down a ladder, while holding on to the stair above.

10 walking backward This skill is usually developed at around age two.

11 running Between 18 and 24 months, most toddlers become proficient runners, though they are prone to tripping and running into things.

12 jumping By age two and a half, most toddlers can jump with both feet, though skipping will take another two years or more.

first-aid kit essentials

having the items you need on hand can make a big difference when an accident or illness occurs. Keep these supplies (except the ice pack) in a locked storage area out of your child's reach. Medications must also be stored away from excess humidity (not in the bathroom's medicine cabinet). Make sure that anyone who's watching your child knows where to find the materials and how to use them. Your at-home kit should include:

tools and sterilizers:

1 an infant/child thermometer For infants, you'll need a rectal thermometer; for toddlers, either a rectal or a digital ear model.

2 tweezers For removing splinters and ticks.

3 sharp scissors For cutting bandages.

4 a calibrated cup or spoon or an oral syringe For measuring and administering liquid medications.

5 a heating pad or hot-water bottle For soothing upset tummies.

6 an ice pack For applying to bruises and sprains. (A bag of frozen vegetables is a terrific substitute.)

7 a small high-beam flashlight For checking sore throats and getting a good look at eyes, ears, noses, and splinter areas.

8 tongue depressors To check sore throats. (A flat lollipop is a fun substitute for older toddlers and kids.)

9 nasal bulb syringe For unclogging stuffed noses.

10 rubbing alcohol For sterilizing the thermometer and other tools.

11 petroleum jelly To lubricate rectal thermometers.

12 gloves For handling blood

medications and topical treatments:

13 pain reliever A non-aspirin, infant's- or children's-strength acetaminophen or ibuprofen. Be extremely careful to follow your doctor's or the manufacturer's dosage recommendations since overdosing can lead to severe liver damage.

14 antihistamine Such as Benadryl, in case of allergic reaction to a sting.

15 rehydration fluids Such as Pedialyte, to treat dehydration.

16 syrup of ipecac and activated charcoal These are used in cases of accidental poisoning. But never give your child a poison remedy without first checking with your local poison-control center, since using them incorrectly can cause further damage.

17 hydrogen peroxide To clean cuts and scrapes.

18 antibacterial cream For applying to cuts and scrapes after cleansing.

19 calamine lotion or hydrocortisone cream For soothing the itch of insect bites or rashes caused by poison ivy, poison oak, or sumac.

20 child-strength insect repellent For applying to clothing and some skin areas before seasonal outdoor activity.

21 sunscreen Use only baby or children's varieties.

bandages and wipes:

22 gauze For dressing wounds (it won't stick to tender skin). Have both rolls (an inch or two wide) and pads (2-by-2-inch and 4-by-4-inch) on hand.

23 adhesive tape For applying gauze.

24 sterile cotton balls For washing small cuts and bruises.

25 cotton swabs For cleaning the outside areas of noses and ears. Never insert a swab into a child's nose, which could cause any foreign matter to be pushed upward into the sinus cavity, nor use a swab to clean deeply into a child's ear, which removes the protective wax and can harm the eardrum.

26 adhesive bandage strips Have a variety of sizes and shapes on hand. However, never put a bandage strip on a young child's fingers or any area that might be sucked on, since it presents a choking hazard.

27 ace bandage

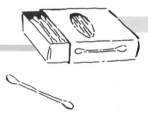

childproofing

your child's curiosity will propel her to grow intellectually and emotionally, but it will also lead her into harm's way. Many of the accidents that could befall her are avoidable. In addition to your room-by-room childproofing, be sure to:

1 have smoke detectors and carbon monoxide detectors Install them on each level of the house and replace batteries twice a year.

2 routinely check your water supply If you have a well, check it once a year for contaminants, including lead. Also be sure the well has a secure cap and cover. Periodically check water from a public source, as well. Keep bottled water on hand in the event of a health alert from your water supplier. Boil water for use by newborns.

3 check your home for unseen contaminants Have your home checked for radon. If your home was built before 1980, check the paint on walls for lead. Old painted furniture and imported painted dishware should also be checked for lead. Check the soil, too, for pesticide residue and lead. Hire a qualified professional if you need to do any renovations that might release asbestos into the air.

4 conduct regular household safety checks As your child's abilities grow, so do her chances of getting into trouble. Don't wait until your child is walking to childproof areas of your home that are seemingly impossible for your child to reach. Remember: You need to literally stay one step ahead of your baby, always anticipating the next surge in development.

5 conduct seasonal household safety checks Before winter, have your chimney and heating system professionally checked. Clean and if necessary replace air-conditioning filters in the spring, rather than waiting for the first heat spell.

6 protect your child from falls Falls are the number-one cause of injury to young children. Take a survey of all falling hazards in your home and minimize the danger. Remove scatter rugs, which can trip a new walker. Cushion sharp-edged furniture corners. Install safety gates at the tops and bottoms of stairs. Always use the safety harness on the high chair and changing table, don't leave your baby—even for a few seconds—alone on a bed or other high surface, and be sure that windows have protective bars. Don't use walkers, which allow your child to zip around a room without the benefit of being able to see her feet and the ground.

7 beware of glass Young children don't have the experience to know that what they can see beyond glass isn't within their grasp. So, place decals or other visual aids on sliding glass doors and on windows to alert your child to the presence of a barrier.

8 avoid burns Adjust the thermostat on your water heater so that water never exceeds 120 degrees F. Always use the back burners of the stove and always turn pot handles inward so your curious toddler will not be tempted to reach for a visible pot handle. Never cook your child's food in the microwave, which results in super-hot spots in the food or formula and can lead to scalding. Never leave a hot iron where your child can reach it or its cord, and avoid ironing when your child is nearby. Also avoid electrical burns from outlets by putting in outlet covers.

9 watch out for water hazards Children can drown in just an inch of water. Never leave cleaning buckets filled with water where your child has access to them. Never leave your child unsupervised, even for a few seconds, in the bath, and install safety latches on toilet seats. If you have a pool, be sure that it is surrounded by a locked fence through which your child cannot enter.

10 safely store all potentially harmful items Cleaning products, medicines, buttons, coins—any items that your child could ingest—need to be kept out of reach and locked in a secure place.

11 restrict especially hazardous areas From the time your child is crawling, make sure that dangerous areas of your home are off-limits with doors that cannot be opened by your toddler. These areas include the laundry room, the bathroom, the garage, and any terrace or loft area.

12 be vigilant The most important safety rule is to keep your child under constant supervision.

bedroom basics

In addition to ensuring that individual items are safe, it's important to take an overall approach to safety in your child's room. Here's what to look for:

1 all furniture should be sturdy and untippable Secure shelving units, dressers, and other freestanding items to the wall.

2 lock drawers, doors, and cabinets Install safety latches on all storage items that your child should not have access to.

3 cover radiators and electrical outlets Make sure any heat sources have guards around them to keep your child from touching them and burning himself. Place covers over all electrical sockets.

4 don't entice your child to danger Never place attractive toys on high shelves, which could encourage him to climb, or leave drawers open, which could encourage him to step into them.

5 check dresser knobs for safety Dresser knobs should be too large to swallow and too small to provide a climbing foothold. They should also be attached securely and designed not to be easily pulled by a young child.

6 pad sharp edges Specially designed corner cushion guards help prevent injuries. Don't simply tape foam or other materials to the corners of sharp furniture since it can present a choking hazard.

7 store toys conveniently Keep toys either in an easily accessible place or out of sight. If you use a toy box, choose one without a lid.

8 choose window treatments wisely Avoid curtains that can be pulled down. Tie or remove dangling window-shade and window-blind cords. Install a window guard at the bottom of the window.

parents ALERT!

If there's an older sibling or friend in the house who has toys with small parts, be careful to keep these away from your younger child, who could choke on them.

crib safety checklist

Whether you're purchasing a new crib or using a hand-me-down, be sure it meets these safety standards:

1 there are no more than 2³/8 inches between the crib slats And no slats are missing, broken, or loose.

2 all the hardware should be secure

3 the mattress must fit snugly No more than two of your fingers should fit between the edge of the mattress and the side of the crib.

4 no posts should extend over 1/16 of an inch And no cutout designs in the headboard or footboard.

5 crib material must be smooth and nontoxic Don't use a crib manufactured before 1980, which may contain lead paint. There should be no peeling or cracked paint, and no splinters or rough edges.

things to know about your child's bedding

When you put your baby down for a nap or at bed-time, you'll rest much easier yourself if you know that his crib environment is as safe as it can be.

1 crib materials should not be able to smother
If bumper pads are used, they should fit around the entire crib, and have at least six straps (one at each corner and one on each long side of the crib) securing them in place. The ties that hold the bumpers should not be long enough that your child can chew on them or entangle a finger or toe. Remove all pillows, thick quilts, heavy blankets, and toys from the crib while your child is in the crib. If you're concerned about the cold, dress your baby in a blanket sleeper. Use only heavyweight, rubberlike mattress protectors. Never use thin, trash-bag-weight plastic coverings on the mattress, which can cling to your child's face and suffocate him.

2 never use plush materials Children under age one should never sleep on plush materials such as a waterbed, heavy quilt, beanbag-type chair, pillow, or lambskin, since they can easily suffocate.

3 use cotton or synthetic bedding Especially if your child has allergies, or if your family has a history of allergies. Wool fibers are more likely to produce aller-gic reactions in susceptible kids. If your child is severely allergic, encase the mattress in covers designed to reduce or eliminate allergens.

4 place your child's bed in a safe spot It should be away from radiators, heating vents, lamps, or other plugged-in appliances, windows, and especially away from window-shade or window-blind cords.

5 never hang objects from the crib or bed Never tie a toy or an item such as a laundry bag from the bedpost or crib slats, since the string could pose a risk of strangulation.

6 adjust the bedding as your child grows Once your child can stand up, adjust the mattress to its lowest position and remove the bumper pads, which can now be used as a climbing platform. Once your child is about 35 inches tall or has begun to climb, it's time to move him into a bed or simply to place the crib mattress on the floor before making the transition to a bed.

7 choose a toddler bed with care Whether your child is moving to a toddler bed or an adult-size bed, make sure it's sturdy, and like the crib, has no posts or cutouts that could be dangerous, and that it's positioned safely in the room. Until the transition is complete, place soft cushions or quilts on the floor to reduce the risk of injury if your child should fall out of the bed. Never allow a child under the age of six to sleep in the top bunk of a bunkbed.

changing table rules

While inevitably some diaper changes will take place in the crib or on the floor, your best bet for your baby's safety and your own comfort is to have a changing table designed for this purpose. When choosing and using a changing table:

1 get a sturdy table with a built-in safety strap Always use the strap to restrain your baby whenever she's on the table. Never leave your baby unattended, even while strapped in.

2 opt for a two-inch lip around all four edges This provides an extra precaution against falls.

3 keep supplies and clothing in easy reach Choose a dresser combo or a style with open shelving beneath the table, which works well.

playpen safety

When your baby has a small area in which to play safely, you can get needed work done without fear of him getting underfoot. However, it's important to bring the same careful scrutiny to using a playpen or play yard as you do any environment in which you place your baby. Make sure that:

1 netting has a small weave without any tears
The weave should be so small that not even your baby's finger could slip through and become entwined.

2 the drop side is up and securely locked
Whenever he is inside, your baby can roll into the pocket created between the mesh and the playpen pad and suffocate. Also, he could crawl or climb out of the playpen if all the sides are not locked up or could catch his fingers in the hinges.

3 the rails and padding are in good condition
Do not use a playpen in which the padded rails have rips or tears. Your child could remove and ingest the plastic material.

4 never string toys from the playpen
Any dangling string or cord puts your child at risk of strangulation.

5 don't put large toys, pillows, or other climbable objects inside
Standing on these types of things could encourage your child to try to climb out, resulting in a tumble.

6 never use an accordion-style fence as a play yard
A child can get his head caught in the openings or injure his fingers on hinges.

kitchen hazards

for young children, the kitchen is a compelling place: There are pots and pans to rattle, the lights and action of so many appliances, and, most of all, the likelihood that a grown-up will be doing something interesting, such as lighting the stove or opening and closing the refrigerator. For all its wonder, the kitchen poses particular dangers to your child. To keep your child safe:

1 take care of appliances Use cord shorteners to make sure that no cords are dangling within your baby's reach. Unplug appliances such as the toaster and coffeemaker when not in use. Cover all electrical sockets that are not in use with safety caps. Install safety latches on refrigerators and stoves and other appliances that can be opened. Remove or cover stove knobs to ensure that your child cannot accidentally turn them on.

2 lock drawers, cabinets, and cupboards Install safety latches on anything that opens. Even if the items inside pose no particular risk, toddlers can pinch their fingers in doors and drawers.

3 store dangerous items out of reach Items that do pose a risk, such as cleaning products and alcohol, should be stored on an out-of-reach shelf to eliminate any risk when you unlatch a cabinet door. Nontoxic items, too, such as aluminum foil boxes with sharp serrated blades, and pointy-tipped utensils need to be safely stored.

4 keep spices out of reach Nutmeg and bay leaves may be toxic. (See page 87.)

5 remove trash safely Use a child-resistant garbage can. Or keep trash behind a cabinet with a safety latch. Whether you're tossing or storing plastic bags, tie a knot in each one to prevent a possible suffocation hazard.

6 consider the unlikely possible Before your child came into the world, you probably never had to worry about such unlikely possibilities as the stove tipping over. Yet, a toddler who opens an oven door and stands on it can, indeed, cause it—and other heavy equipment—to tip. If it can be climbed on, it can topple, unless it is secured to the wall. Look around and consider other dangerous events that a curious toddler could set in motion: climbing into a refrigerator; falling on a hot oven door; sticking a hand, foot, or toy into the garbage disposal; falling atop an open dishwasher drawer that holds knives. (Place knives and other sharp objects sharp-side down in the dishwasher.) Use your imagination before your toddler uses hers.

make your eating area safer

Sitting around the table for family meals provides your child with more than physical nourishment. The dinner table is where he'll learn social skills and enjoy the company of the adults in his life. To be sure that your eating area is safe:

1 forego tablecloths Tablecloths make it too easy for your child to haul the contents of the table down onto himself. Opt for rigid placemats that can't easily be moved.

2 keep chairs securely under the table Chairs that protrude out from the table when not in use make a perfect staircase for your toddler to reach the table.

3 brace tables securely Pedestal-style tables can topple over onto a child who puts too much weight on the table's edge. Be sure to keep chairs under pedestal tables and to teach your child never to lean on or hang from the table's edge. Folding tables and chairs can collapse easily when a child climbs on them and should not be used.

4 store or discard leftovers immediately Your child will no doubt want to sample and play with any tempting foods, drinks, and sharp objects left on the table. Clear the table before removing your child from his high chair.

high-chair pointers

1 opt for one with a wide base It won't easily tilt.

2 avoid styles with decorative posts They can be a strangulation hazard if an item of clothing catches on the post.

3 always use the restraining strap

4 place it far enough away from the table Your child must not be able to reach the tabletop. Also make sure it's far enough away from the walls and other furniture so that your child cannot push or kick the chair over.

5 if you use a toddler seat attached to the table With the kind that attaches to a firmly anchored table, be sure that your child's feet cannot touch a chair. (Some parents mistakenly believe that having an adult-size chair under the booster seat provides an extra level of protection, but it actually poses the risk that the child will stand on the chair and thus detach the booster from the table.)

bathroom safety checks

Long before your child is using the bathroom on her own, you'll need to make sure it is childproofed. It's best to keep the door locked from the outside when the room is not in use. For those times that she is in the bathroom, be sure to:

1 lock up all medicines and cleaning products Medicines should not be stored in the bathroom since humidity can lessen their effectiveness. Keep bathroom cleaning products in a locked cabinet. Both should be kept out of reach—either up high or locked up.

2 adjust the thermostat Set the water heater to a maximum of 120 degrees F.

3 cover floors with nonskid rugs

4 install outlet covers

5 never let a child under five use a whirlpool bath
The powerful jets can overpower a young child, and
the suction can trap her under the water. A child who
puts her head underwater risks ensnaring her hair, thus
also trapping her underwater.

6 never leave a child alone in the bathroom Ever.
Not for even a moment. It only takes seconds for a
child to drown, even in an inch of water. If you must
leave the room for even a few seconds, take your child
with you.

7 use a toilet seat lock

laundry room checks

Whether your laundry room is a part of the kitchen,
a separate area in the house, or the corner laun-
dromat, it's essential that you be vigilant when your child is
in the laundry area.

1 lock appliance doors Toddlers see adventure in
climbing into washers and dryers.

2 secure front-loading appliances to the wall If
your child stands on or climbs onto an open dryer or
washer door, the appliance could topple.

3 turn off appliances when not in use Unplug all
laundry room appliances when you're not using them
and cover the outlets with safely plugs.

4 avoid ironing when your child is around A tug
on an iron's cord could result in severe burns and
other injuries. At least, remember never to leave a hot
iron unattended. Remember that irons stay hot long
after they've been turned off, so place your just-used,
unplugged iron in a safe space (such as inside an
otherwise empty sink) where it can't topple or be
reached by your child.

5 keep soaps and bleaches in a locked cabinet

steps to stair safety

I t's a momentous occasion when your child finally masters the art of stair climbing. Getting the hang of it takes time, and toddlers, in their rush to get from here to there, are neither patient or proficient enough to handle stairs safely on their own. To keep your child safe as he handles life's ups and downs:

1 install safety gates Put gates at the tops and bottoms of all accessible stairs

2 install low railings if possible Once your child has the basics of stair climbing under his belt, he'll want to handle the adventure on his own. An easy-to-reach handrail can help keep him safe.

3 repair any torn carpet on the stairs Or replace it. A child's small foot can snag in places that adults wouldn't find dangerous.

4 check banisters for safety The slats of the banister railings should be sturdy, positioned vertically, and no more than 3½ inches apart to avoid any risk of entrapment or slipping through. Banisters that do not meet these standards should be removed and replaced or covered over with balcony/deck netting. Remove any posts, which pose a strangulation hazard.

5 keep stairs free of obstacles Don't store items on stairs. In addition to presenting the risk of tripping, kids can stand on items such as chairs on stair landings, and topple over the banisters.

6 close open-backed stairs Basement stairs particularly often have an open-back design, as do spiral staircases. The backs should be covered securely to prevent a child from slipping through and strangling between the steps.

common furniture hazards

furniture is designed with adult comfort in mind. And, for kids, some items pose real dangers. For instance:

1 bookshelves can topple To young climbers, open bookshelves represent a particularly appealing challenge. Anchor them to the wall to prevent tipping and don't store anything in plain sight that your child must not touch.

2 dresser drawers can make a fun staircase Leaving a drawer open for even a moment can entice a child to climb into it either to see what's inside or to reach items on the dresser top. On some dressers, the knobs are large enough to provide a good foothold. To protect your child, lock the drawers and replace climbable drawer pulls with flat ones.

3 glass breaks Consider putting your glass-topped coffee table and shelving in storage for a few years. Or replace the glass with unbreakable plastic for now.

4 soft surfaces can smother Infants, particularly, are at risk of suffocation when placed on soft sofa cushions, beanbag-type chairs, waterbeds, thick quilts, and sheepskins. Lay babies only on firm, flat surfaces.

5 rockers can pinch Brace rocking chairs against a wall when not in use or use blocks underneath to keep them from rocking when your toddler is toddling about. Or consider replacing the traditional-style rocker with a glider. Keep in mind, too, that toddlers who are just learning to walk depend on the stability of furniture.

6 recliners can entrap a child Kids under the age of six or so can become trapped in the footrest of a recliner and be strangled. Place any recliners in your home against the wall so that they cannot open while not in use by an adult.

exercise equipment Keep all exercise equipment out of your child's reach. Bikes, rowers, stair steppers, and other mechanical devices contain a number of gears that could entrap and injure your child. Even two-pound weights, if your child drops one on herself, can be deadly.

heating and air conditioning systems

To keep your house healthy and comfortable:

1 have your heating system inspected annually

Professionl maintenance checks should include making sure that furnaces are crack-free with no missing panels or flue caps; checking air ducts for cracks, to ensure that they are properly insulated and away from flammable objects. Keep a screen around the furnace to prevent kids from tampering with it and from getting burned. Never place objects over it to dry.

2 check fireplace flue and chimney annually

Place a spark screen in front of the fireplace whenever a fire is burning. Keep fireplace tools out of your child's reach. Remove and safely store the key to a gas-fueled fireplace. Never burn treated wood, plastic, or newspapers, which release toxic fumes in a wood-burning fireplace. Don't use a wood-burning fireplace if your child has asthma or other respiratory ailment.

3 use space heaters with caution
If you use a kerosene heater, use only clear, grade-A kerosene, and surround it with a spark-stopping screen. An electric model that shuts off automatically is a better choice. Position any heater at least three feet from upholstery, curtains, and other flammable materials. Make sure the cord presents no tripping hazard. Never leave the device unattended or use it while sleeping. Most important, keep children away from it.

4 be wise to air-conditioner dangers Don't over-load the electrical system by installing more than one unit into the same outlet. Be sure that any unit extending outside a window or from the wall of the house is positioned in such a way that your child won't bump into it or be tempted to climb onto it. Install a fence or rounded-edged cage around it. At least twice a year (if used year-round) or seasonally, change the filters and clean the ducts.

make electrical appliances safe

In addition to making sure that large appliances such as washers and refrigerators are locked, that cords don't dangle, and that appliances are unplugged when not in use:

1 firmly anchor most appliances Or place them off-limits to your child. TVs must be placed on sturdy surfaces, not TV carts. VCRs and DVD players should have special locks to keep kids from sticking their hands inside.

2 follow manufacturer's guidelines faithfully
Never try to bypass safety features, and never exceed the wattage of a lightbulb in a lamp. Doing so could result in a fire.

3 don't use plug-in appliances near water

4 use appliances only as intended Restrict them to their intended purpose and intended users. Electric blankets, which are designed for adults, are extremely unsafe for children.

5 be cautious with cords and extension cords
Never use a lightweight extension cord for a heavy-duty appliance. Never run a cord under a rug, where it can overheat, or around a doorway, where it can fray. Replace frayed cords immediately.

fire safety rules

In spite of years of decreasing death rates from fires, fire continues to be the number-one household hazard. To keep your family and your home safe:

1 install smoke detectors on each level And check them regularly. Replace the batteries twice a year—each time you change the clock to and from daylight savings time. Consider installing automatic fire sprinklers in areas where a fire could otherwise get a head start, such as the basement and attic.

2 inspect all heating and electrical devices Regularly repair or replace any items that become overheated, that have frayed wiring, or that have any indications of short circuitry. Maintain all heating system components.

3 use caution when cooking Nearly half of all house fires begin in the kitchen. Never leave foods cooking unattended. Do not have curtains on windows near the stove. Keep paper towels, oven mitts, food containers, and all other flammable items away from the stove.

4 watch for cigarette, pipe, and cigar hazards Never smoke in bed or while drowsy or allow anyone in your home to do so. Use caution when disposing of any smoking materials. Douse all cigarettes and matches in water before putting them into the trash.

5 keep fire tools out of kids' reach Lock matches and lighters in a safe place.

6 limit the storage of flammable liquids And keep storage areas free from flammable debris. Never store gasoline in your home. Store other flammables in their original containers or in safety containers in a locked area away from heat sources. Don't allow old newspapers and magazines and other combustibles to gather in basements and attics.

7 have a proper fire extinguisher accessible

A good multipurpose extinguisher marked "ABC" should be positioned for easy access by an adult. Never use water or a type "A" extinguisher (designed for putting out fires from combustibles such as wood and paper) on an electrical or grease fire.

8 keep appliance areas clean

Dirt buildup around a dishwasher or lint buildup in a dryer vent can cause a fire. Be sure to clean areas around heat-producing appliances regularly.

9 be especially watchful during holidays

And when entertaining. Candles and holiday lights should never be left glowing when you're out of the room.

10 have a fire escape plan

Regularly review with your children what to do in case of fire. Kids should know how to exit the building and what escape dangers to avoid, such as opening a door that's hot to the touch. They should be taught to crawl beneath smoke rather than attempt to run through it.

parents ALERT!

stop, drop, and roll if clothing catches fire Children, even as young as age three, can be taught the three-step rule in the event of a clothing fire: Stop, drop, and roll. The child should stop immediately, since running fans the flames. He should drop to the ground, and roll around to smother the flames.

no smoking Do not to smoke in a household with children because it increases their risk of respiratory infections.

Your backyard offers your child a world of fun. To keep the fun safe:

1 barbecue with extreme care Choose sturdy and reliable outdoor cooking equipment and store it in a locked shed when not in use. Use barbecue grills only in well-ventilated outdoor areas, and never in a garage or other indoor space, even with the door open, since carbon monoxide builds up rapidly. Also keep the grill away from overhanging trees, or windows where the smoke could enter your home. Always follow the manufacturer's guidelines in the use of the grill and fuel. Store fuels and cooking utensils safely out of your child's reach. If possible, fence in a barbecue area to restrict your child's access to it.

2 check decks and porches for safety As with staircases, remove any protruding posts, check that deck slats are vertical and no more than 3½ inches apart, and be sure that the railing around a porch is sturdy, high enough to prevent a child from toppling over it, and that no climbable furniture is nearby. Enclose the back of an open-backed outdoor staircase to prevent the risk of entrapment.

3 beware of glass hazards If you have a sliding glass door, place decals at your child's eye level to alert him to the presence of the glass. Use only non-breakable, plastic tableware for outdoor eating.

4 limit water hazards See "How to Make Your Outdoor Pool Safer," pages 66–67.

5 have your child wear shoes Any time your child is outdoors, even on a well-manicured lawn, have her wear shoes. Any discarded material, a built-in sprinkler, or even natural debris such as acorn pods, can hurt tender feet.

6 be careful around backyard play equipment Choose sturdy, age-appropriate playsets, not swings and climbers that your child will grow into. Be sure to position the equipment safely in the yard, far enough away from walls, fences, trees, and high-traffic areas (such as next to your outdoor dining area) to avoid collisions. Periodically check the equipment for wear, and repair or replace any jagged, splintering, cracked, or otherwise damaged pieces. Be sure that the ground area around the play yard allows for safe landings. There should be a soft surface, loose sand or mulch about 12 inches deep, or special foam or rubber mats designed for playgrounds.

7 be watchful in garages and driveways Never let your child play around automatic garage doors or use the remote to open and close the doors. If possible, separate the driveway from the outdoor play area with a sturdy fence. If your child is not in the car with you, make sure that another adult is supervising her as you pull out of the driveway. Get in the habit of walking around your car before getting in to make sure that play equipment—or even your child—is not behind the car. Honk or call out to any child you think might be in the area before pulling out. Also, always lock cars when not in use because children can climb in and engage the car.

8 use caution when gardening Follow the manufacturer's directions when using any chemicals on your lawn. Keep your child away from the lawn for twice the time suggested by the manufacturer. Store all gardening chemicals in a locked place out of your child's reach. Do not use these chemicals while your child is gardening with you.

9 store equipment and supplies wisely Lay ladders on their sides rather than storing them upright, which could entice your child to climb. Lay rakes with tines down. Store pesticides, fertilizer, and other hazardous materials in a locked, ventilated area.

10 never use motor-driven machines near kids Keep your children indoors when you use motor-powered equipment. Nearly 8,000 kids are injured each year in the United States in lawnmower-related accidents. Children should never ride on mowers, nor should they be in the yard while you're using any power mowers or power tools such as hedge cutters or power saws.

11 be aware of dangers from common items

Store hoses properly after each use to avoid tripping hazards. String clotheslines out of your child's reach. Install a ground fault circuit interrupter to avoid electrical shock. Be sure that yard fencing material is free of rust, splinters, and other hazards and that it cannot be climbed or opened by a toddler. Keep the garbage can inaccessible.

12 keep a wireless phone with you in the yard

In case of an accident you want to be able to get help immediately and not have to leave your injured child to go inside for a phone.

how to make your outdoor pool safer

to help your pool remain the pleasurable place it's meant to be:

1 closely supervise your child at all times
Never leave your child near a pool without an adult who can swim.

2 prevent access when not in use
Make sure that your child and other kids cannot get near the water on their own. Install a fence that cannot be climbed around the entire perimeter of the pool, and make sure that the gate latches securely. Remove ladders that enable easy access to the water of an aboveground pool. And always drain wading pools when not in use.

3 never rely on inflatable toys or water wings
They are not designed to keep your child safe.

4 never put your child in a stroller or walker

These are dangerous anywhere near an in-ground pool. Even if you're right there and the stroller or walker lands in the pool, it could be impossible for you to retrieve your child in time.

5 always have a phone poolside To save precious

seconds in case of emergency.

6 know your child's abilities in the water Don't

go into the water with an infant who cannot yet hold his head upright on his own, an ability that usually comes at about four to five months of age. Make sure the water temperature is at least 84 degrees F for infants under six months. Older babies and toddlers should only be in water that's at least 78 degrees F. Kids should come out of the water after about half an hour or sooner if they show signs of being cold.

7 don't allow children to drink pool water

Untreated water could contain microbes that could make your baby sick. Treated water contains chemicals that could also harm your child.

8 dress babies and toddlers in swim diapers

This will prevent leakage of bowel movements. But remember that such diapers do not completely prevent the dispersal of fecal bacteria if he has a bowel movement. If any child has a bowel movement in the pool, have all people leave the pool immediately and replace and treat the water appropriately to prevent infection with *E. coli,* a bacterium that can be life-threatening in small children.

9 don't let your child swim after tummy distress

You should never allow a child to swim within a week of a bout of diarrhea or other gastrointestinal disease.

health and hygiene routines

hygiene habits for toddlers

While a young child certainly isn't ready to take on the task of keeping herself healthy, even a toddler can learn these hygiene basics:

1 wash hands Always wash before eating and after using the toilet. Hand contact is the number-one way to spread germs.

2 cough and sneeze into a tissue if possible If a tissue isn't readily available, tell her to direct a cough or sneeze into the crook of her arm rather than into her hands or into the air.

3 blow the nose Once your child is about 18 months old, she can begin to learn the fine art of nose blowing. Let her practice by blowing onto a tissue and making it move.

4 don't share personal-hygiene products Teach your child to use only her own comb, brush, and toothbrush.

5 don't share food or eating utensils

6 put nothing but food into your mouth By toddlerhood, you can begin to curb your child's oral explorations.

ways to limit diaper rash

even the most well-cared-for baby can occasionally get diaper rash. And some babies are more prone to it than others. To limit the occurrence:

1 choose the right diapers Disposables tend to keep your baby's bottom dryer, thus limiting the damp environment in which bacteria thrive. If your baby develops a rash, consider switching brands until you find one that seems right for him.

2 change your baby often Change your baby's diaper immediately after a bowel movement or if his diaper is soaked, and don't let him languish longer than half an hour in a damp diaper.

3 watch the fit A too-tight diaper can trap moisture.

4 watch the diet Drinking too much fruit juice or eating acidic foods can make the urine more acidic, leading to a rash.

5 avoid overcleaning Overuse of wipes and soaps can cause rashes. Much of the time, a soft damp cloth is all you'll need to clean your baby's bottom.

6 expose your baby's bottom to the air When possible, let your child go for a while without a diaper. Immediately after removing a soiled diaper is usually a good time since it's less likely that your child will urinate or have another bowel movement right away.

7 treat minor rashes Use ointment containing zinc oxide (or other salve recommended by your pediatrician) before a minor rash becomes a larger, more serious one.

parents ALERT!

talc warning Never shake talcum powder directly on your baby's bottom. Inhalation of the powder can cause respiratory problems. If you use talc, sprinkle it on your hand before applying it to your baby's bottom. Limit or avoid talc on baby girls because its use has been associated with cervical cancer in later life. To help dry your baby's rash, opt for ointments or cornstarch-based powders.

treating diaper rash

o soothe your baby's sore bottom if a rash does
occur:

1 soak her bottom in tepid water Avoid using
soaps, which can further irritate skin. If soaking isn't
possible, use a sterile cotton ball soaked in warm
water to clean her bottom. If touching seems to hurt,
use a spray-mist bottle to gently wash away feces and
to ease discomfort.

2 avoid baby wipes These are fine for quick
cleanups when your baby doesn't have a rash. But
some of the ingredients in commercial wipes can
sting when your child's bottom is sore.

3 use ointment Diaper rash remedies do work.
Ask your baby's doctor for recommendations. You
may need to experiment to see which brand works
best for your child.

4 watch what she wears Cut away the elasticized
leg opening of disposable diapers to allow air to circu-
late freely. Avoid nonbreathable fabrics in clothing
during a rash, and dress your baby in cotton. Wash
all clothing in nonperfumed soap or detergent. When
possible, let your child go diaperless.

5 see your pediatrician If rash persists or is
severe, visit your doctor.

bad habits

It's a rare child who doesn't pick up one or more annoying and potentially harmful habits. Here's how to deal with them:

1 thumb sucking Don't discourage babies from this self-soothing activity. Offer older toddlers hand-held toys or activities to distract them, such as suggesting that they build a block tower or draw a picture. Start a conversation; after all, it's nearly impossible to talk with your thumb in your mouth.

2 nail biting Offer a small toy to squeeze, such as a squishy ball, which, like nail biting, eases tension. Keep your child's nails well manicured, since irregular nails are more tempting to chew.

3 nose picking Offer a tissue or a reminder to blow. Suggest that she pick her nose in private.

4 head banging Give your child another outlet for the release of excess energy, such as a toy drum to bang on.

5 rocking in place Play music and encourage your child to dance with the beat.

6 hair twirling Invest in a long-haired doll, whose hair your child can play with. Also consider getting your child a shorter haircut or styling it in braids or a ponytail to give her less access to it.

seasonal health and safety

warm-weather warnings

playing outdoors in the warm weather is a childhood delight. To keep your child's health glowing while the sun's rays are strongest:

1 practice sunburn prevention See opposite page.

2 provide extra liquids Offer your infant extra breast milk or formula. Offer your toddler or older child eight ounces of noncarbonated liquid (preferably water) every half hour. Dilute fruit juice with water, because sugar slows fluid absorption.

3 never leave your child in a hot car You should never leave your child alone in a car, period. When the outside temperature is over 80 degrees F, it can take less than three minutes for the temperature inside the car to soar to over 100 degrees F—even with the windows partially open—leading to potential heat exhaustion and death.

4 check conflicts of medicines with heat or sun Antihistamines slow down sweat production, raising the risk of heatstroke. Some antibiotics and cortisone products make a child extremely susceptible to sunburn. Ask about possible interactions with medicine.

5 avoid insect bites and stings Whenever there's a chance your child may come into contact with ticks, bees, and other insects, have him wear light-colored, long-sleeved shirts and pants (with pants legs tucked into socks). Steer clear of infested woods or still bodies of water. Use a repellent containing no more than 10 percent DEET. Your best bet is to choose a spray that you can spray onto the clothing, rather than directly on your child's skin. Avoid sweet-scented soaps and shampoos that could attract insects. Seek first aid immediately if he appears to have any allergic reaction to a bite or sting such as difficulty breathing, profuse sweating, or excessive swelling.

6 watch out for overcooled air Your home should be comfortable, not chilly. Bring a lightweight sweater for your child when going to public places that may be too highly air-conditioned.

sunburn blockers

Young children's skin is particularly sensitive to the damage from the sun's ultraviolet light. It takes less than 15 minutes of exposure to cause a burn. To minimize your child's risk of sunburn:

1 seek out shade Avoid playing outdoors in direct sunlight during the peak sunburn hours—from 10 A.M. to 3 P.M. There's no need to keep your child indoors, but opt for play spaces that are shielded from direct rays, such as under trees or beach umbrellas.

2 dress to cover Your child should wear a hat with a wide brim (to protect her face and scalp) and neck protector as well as a tee shirt, and if temperature permits, long pants when outdoors during peak sunburn hours. At the beach or pool, have her wear a light-colored tee shirt and loose pants over her bathing suit.

3 use sunscreen The American Academy of Pediatrics recommends that all children, including infants, wear sunscreen on exposed skin when in sunlight. Use sunscreen with a sun protection factor (SPF) of at least 15, and choose a brand specifically designed for kids. Apply the sunscreen at least 30 minutes before going outdoors, and reapply as needed.

4 supply sunglasses Get your child in the habit of wearing UV-protective glasses early, since heavy exposure to the sun can cause eye damage. Many child-friendly, flexible plastic models are available—and most kids delight in the opportunity to wear them.

5 don't forget lips Apply UV-protective lip balm to your child's lips, too.

winter warnings

Rosy cheeks are the traditional sign of robust health, but winter air can provide too much of a good thing. To be safe and healthy in the cold weather:

1 stay indoors during extreme cold When the temperatures plunge below 5 degrees F or below a wind-chill factor of 0 degrees F, stay indoors. Limit outdoor activities when the temperature is below 20 degrees F.

2 dress warmly, in layers Start by dressing your child in long underwear made of lightweight, breathable fabric like cotton, polypropylene, silk, or other insulating fiber. Layer on a long-sleeved cotton shirt, and then a heavier sweater, flannel shirt, or polarfleece on top. Add a jacket and pants that are waterproof and insulated with down, fleece, or polyester. Make sure your child's head is covered with a snug-fitting hat or hood that covers his ears. Keep hands toasty with lined, waterproof mittens, and tuck feet in two layers of socks—polyester underneath and heavy cotton or wool on top, covered with waterproof lined boots. Shield your child's face from windburn or frostbite with a knit facemask or neck warmer. Avoid scarves, which present a strangulation hazard.

3 change out of wet clothing immediately This will help prevent frostbite.

4 take proper sunburn precautions Winter sun reflects strongly off snow and presents the same sunburn danger as summer sun.

5 provide extra calories and liquids Before and after playing outside on cold days, provide extra foods and beverages. Good choices include hot soup and warm cocoa to help hydrate as well as warm your child.

6 warn against touching or licking metals Warm skin or the tongue can stick to cold metals.

7 insist on safe playing Do not let your child tunnel under snow or play on or near untested frozen bodies of water. Do not allow snowball throwing toward people. Have your child wear a helmet when sledding or skiing.

everyday
routines

feeding and eating

nursing know-how

though nursing is nature's way, nature does not provide everything to make breast-feeding comfortable and convenient. So, you'll need:

1 a nursing bra To ensure the best fit, shop for your nursing bra at around your seventh month of pregnancy, when your breasts are about the size they will be while you are lactating.

2 nursing pads They're useful for catching leaks, especially during the first few weeks after birth.

3 a breast pump and bottles If you're planning to express milk, you'll need either a manual or electric pump. If possible, try out a few models before buying one, since you're likely to have a strong preference for one kind. Opt for opaque plastic over glass bottles since maternal white blood cells, which help your baby fight diseases, tend to cling to glass.

4 front-opening nightgown and shirts Some are designed especially for nursing, for your comfort and your baby's safety. Avoid clothing that has loose buttons or threads that your child could latch on to.

nursing diet

a void alcohol, which can have the same effect on your baby that it does on you. Also, to reduce your baby's risk of developing an allergy, if you have a strong family history of allergies, eliminate these foods from your diet while you are nursing:

1 **peanuts and peanut products**

2 **shellfish**

if your child shows signs of colic, eliminate:

3 **dairy products**

4 **caffeine**

5 **onions**

6 **cabbage**

7 **garlic**

parents ALERT!

clear plastic baby bottles are preferred by many parents over the milky pastels because they are easier to check for cleanliness. However, according to research published by *Consumer Reports,* the clear plastics contain a chemical called bisphenol-A, which can leach into baby's milk, juice, or water. Parents are advised to discard these bottles and to replace them with opaque plastics if you are breast-feeding, glass or opaque plastic if your baby is formula-fed.

time for you: soothing tender breasts

if nursing leaves your breasts feeling sore:

1 avoid tight clothing or ill-fitting bras Wear a carefully fitted nursing bra under comfortable clothes.

2 encourage sucking on a breast with a blocked duct Otherwise, milk will continue to back up and can lead to an infection. If a milk duct develops an abscess or is very painful, or if you show signs of an infection, see your doctor.

3 nurse more often to soothe engorgement If you need to release milk more than your baby needs to eat, use a pump to reduce the milk supply in your breasts.

4 apply warmth Make a warm, moist compress and apply it to tender breasts.

5 lubricate sore nipples with breast milk Your own milk supply is just as effective, if not more so, than commercially available salves. If you do use an ointment, wash breasts before nursing.

6 expose your breasts to air and sunlight If you're able to find a comfortable site for some semi-nude sunbathing, this natural cure works wonders for sore nipples.

bottle-feeding essentials

for safety and convenience, keep these necessities and extras on hand:

1 bottles Glass bottles and opaque, dishwasher-safe plastic bottles are equally good for formula-feedings.

Newborns generally start off with four-ounce bottles, but you can save money by investing in eight-ounce bottles (which will be used later) and filling them only halfway.

2 nipples Look for models that most resemble breast nipples, and experiment until you find one your baby likes. Always discard nipples at the first sign of wear.

3 a bottle brush or bottle liners You'll need a bottle brush to clean bottles unless you're exclusively using bottles with disposable liners.

4 bottle warmer Electric warmers are particularly helpful for late night feedings and can be kept beside your bed for your convenience. Insulated thermal bags are good for storing bottles in the diaper bag during daily outings.

adding solids to baby's diet

going from an all-liquid diet to one that includes solid foods is a major milestone in your baby's life—one that begins at about five or six months of age for most infants. Here's how to get your suckling babe to sample solid treats:

1 never put cereal or other solids in a bottle Mixing solid food with breast milk or formula impairs your child's ability to learn to swallow solids correctly.

2 never mix raw egg with your child's food Eggs may contain salmonella bacteria.

3 start with iron-fortified infant cereal Mix it with breast milk or formula in a bowl. Rice is the preferred first food because it has virtually no allergens.

4 introduce one new food at a time During this process, feed your baby one new food every three to five days so that you can watch for any sensitivity.

5 move on to vegetables and fruits Some doctors recommend introducing vegetables first because babies prefer the sweetness of fruits and it may be more difficult to move on to veggies. You'll also find that your child probably prefers orange vegetables such as carrots to green ones, which are less sweet. Pureed fruits are always a favorite, but it's best to avoid tomatoes, oranges, and grapefruit and juices made from these fruits, since they are highly acidic and can lead to tummy upset and diaper rash.

6 add meat for protein Prepared baby food is the best way to work meat into the diet until babies can chew. Some people prefer holding off on meat until their babies can gum or chew tiny pieces of chicken or turkey.

7 experiment with finger foods Once your child is about six- or seven-months old, introduce bits of dry cereal, such as Cheerios, or teething biscuits to allow her to practice grasping and chewing.

great finger foods

feeding himself gives your child a tremendous sense of satisfaction. He not only sates his appetite, he gets to handle what he's about to eat, getting pleasure and knowledge about textures as well as tastes. When choosing finger foods, remember that safety comes first: Avoid most raw veggies and fruits and chewy breads, such as bagels, until your child has his molars and has lots of practice chewing. Also avoid "airy" snacks that young kids can inhale, such as rice cakes, and sticky foods such as peanut butter that can catch in the throat. Fun finger foods include:

1 cheerios These and other cereals give your child practice manipulating small objects—and dissolve easily on his tongue.

2 small cheese cubes or strips Cheese is soft and very appealing—especially American or muenster cheese.

3 vegetables Serve well-cooked peas, beans, and carrots cut into strips; corn served on the cob (so he can hold it and bite off kernels which are otherwise too small to pick up); avocado; baked sweet potatoes or squash cut into chunks. Canned vegetables with no salt are a good bet because they're nice and soft.

4 fruit Serve diced, without the skin. Apples can be baked. Bananas should be ripe and cut lengthwise; grapes peeled and halved; ripe, soft melon should be served in small chunks. Try to limit citrus at first because it can be too acidic. And avoid strawberries for the first year. Afterwards, limit them as they contain histamines and could cause an allergic reaction.

5 pasta Make shapes your child can pick up—fusilli (corkscrews), for example—and thoroughly cook it before serving plain, or sprinkled with cheese. Opt for whole-grain or spinach noodles, which are more nutritious than those made from white flour. Tortellini or ravioli can be cut in half for a treat.

6 toast Serve with apple butter or cream cheese.

learning to drink from a cup

Whether your child is moving to a cup from your breast or from a bottle, the transition is a momentous—and potentially messy—one. Most babies are ready for the event by the time they're about nine months old. To make it easier:

1 look for a weighted bottom and spouted lid
These specially made toddler cups come complete with two handles for easier grasping.

2 demonstrate Watching you drink—from her cup or from your own—will encourage your baby to imitate.

3 start small Until your baby has the hang of it, fill the cup with only an ounce or two of liquid.

4 offer a familiar drink Expressed breast milk, formula, or water are good beginning beverages.

5 make it fun Introduce the cup during mealtimes or when your baby can experiment with the cup yet still satisfy her hunger or thirst in a more familiar way. Don't introduce the cup as a substitute for the familiar bottle or breast when your child is hungry and more likely to be easily frustrated, or at bedtime, when she'll prefer the comfort of her old routine.

a diet for one-year-olds

between the ages of one and two, your child needs 900 to 1,400 calories a day, which should include a variety of foods from each of the major food groups. Served at regular mealtimes along with three or four snacks a day, a nutritious diet includes:

- **4–6 servings of grains** Each serving might include ½ slice of bread; ¼ cup of cooked pasta, rice, beans, or legumes; or 1 ounce of cereal.
- **4–6 servings of fruits and vegetables** Each serving can include ¼ cup of cooked broccoli, peas, spinach, carrots, corn, or other vegetables; half of a fruit; or ½ cup of chopped or cooked fruit.
- **4 servings of dairy** ½ cup of whole milk or yogurt or an ounce of cheese is one serving.
- **2–4 servings of protein** One egg; 2 ounces of meat, fish, or poultry; or 2½ ounces of tofu constitute one serving.

parents ALERT!

don't limit fat in your baby's diet Unlike adults, young kids need a diet that contains fat to ensure proper physical and mental growth. Don't replace whole milk or cheese with low-fat varieties until your child has reached the age of two.

what two- and three-year-olds should eat

at ages two and three, your child needs 900 to 1,700 calories a day. During these years, your child will likely have strong preferences for certain foods and a clear disdain for others. While respecting your child's tastes, be sure to offer a nutritious variety daily, including:

- **6 servings of grains** Each serving might include 1 slice of bread; ½ cup of cooked pasta, rice, beans, or legumes; or 1 to 2 ounces of cereal.
- **6 servings of fruits and vegetables** Each serving can include ¼ cup of cooked broccoli, peas, carrots, corn, or other vegetables; half of a fruit; or ½ cup of chopped or cooked fruit.
- **4 servings of dairy** ½ cup of low-fat milk or yogurt or an ounce of reduced-fat cheese makes one serving.
- **2–4 servings of protein** One egg; 2 ounces of meat, fish, or poultry; or 2½ ounces of tofu constitute one serving.

good eating habits

It's important to establish early on that eating is for nutrition and pleasure; try not to let food and eating rituals become a battleground.

1 let your child set the schedule Babies will eat when they're hungry and stop when they're full. If you think your baby is hungry, offer the breast or a bottle, but don't assume that he is hungry whenever he cries. He may just want to be held or need a diaper change. Let him eat as much as he wants at each feeding, but don't insist that he continue to nurse for a set time or bottle feed until the bottle is empty. If your baby turns away or otherwise indicates that he has had enough, he has. As long as he's gaining weight, you know he's eating enough. Allow your toddler to have small healthy snacks between meals, rather than expecting him to wait until mealtimes.

2 encourage new foods, but don't insist Like adults, children have food preferences. Unlike adults, these preferences can change from one day to the next. Offer new foods whenever possible, but don't insist that he eat an entire meal of never-before-tried foods. Serve a teaspoonful of a new food along with an old favorite to give your child a chance to develop a taste for a wider variety of foods. Remember that you may have to offer a new food a dozen times before your child accepts it.

3 never insist that your child clean his plate

Kids need to learn that food is to satisfy hunger and they shouldn't eat beyond the point of feeling full. Feed your child small portions to avoid waste, allowing him to come back for more if he's still hungry.

4 don't make any food taboo

While you certainly don't want to let your child have a diet of junk food, putting any food, such as candy, completely off-limits only makes it more attractive.

5 each meal doesn't have to be totally nutritious

Don't worry if your child's daily intake leans toward starches one day and fruits the next. What's important is that in the course of a week, he does eat a variety of foods containing the vitamins and minerals he needs.

6 never use food to punish or reward

Don't withhold foods to punish or use food to reward good behavior. It's also important not to make comments such as, "You're a good boy for eating your broccoli." Linking food and behavior with self-worth sets your child up for later eating disorders.

7 respect quirky eating behaviors

But don't go overboard. It's perfectly normal for toddlers to go on food jags, preferring one food above all others or insisting that the foods on his plate can't touch. Don't comment on eating behaviors, since a statement such as "He won't eat anything but tuna fish" can become a self-fulfilling prophecy. At family mealtimes, feed your child some of his preferred food along with the family fare. Invest in a divided plate out of respect for his need to keep foods separate. Don't, however, get in the habit of making your picky eater a separate meal at each lunch and dinner.

8 enlist your child's help in the kitchen

Even toddlers can help wash lettuce for salads or stir the ingredients in a casserole. However, don't let your child touch raw meats or uncooked eggs or eggshells, all of which contain bacteria.

don't eat that!

common foods that can harm your child

because their immune systems are not yet fully functional, certain foods should be avoided by young children, including:

1 honey Children under 12 months should not consume raw honey. Some honey contains spores of *Clostridium botulinum,* an organism that can cause botulism in babies. It's okay for children to eat baked goods containing honey, however.

2 salt Small quantities found in prepared foods do not present a problem. However, ingesting large amounts of table salt or soy sauce can result in salt poisoning or seizures.

3 nutmeg Sprinkling nutmeg on cookies or cakes is fine. Rarely, if a child ingests a quantity of nutmeg, she may experience hallucinations.

4 cooking extracts Pure vanilla and other extracts used in baking contain alcohol. In addition to the alcohol, the extract itself is harmful in large quantities, and ingesting more than a few ounces could lead to central nervous system damage.

5 bay leaves Swallowing these sharp-edged leaves can damage the gastrointestinal tract. Before serving any dish with this spice, remove the leaves.

if there is a strong family history of allergies, you may reduce a child's risk of developing these specific food allergies by not feeding the following to your child:

6 peanuts and peanut butter Peanuts are also a choking hazard.

7 shellfish

choking hazards for kids under age three

Without a full set of molars, babies and toddlers are not yet ready to grind their food as much as needed. To avoid putting your child at risk for choking, don't serve:

1 peanut butter In addition to its potential for causing allergies, peanut butter can "glue" a child's mouth closed or become lodged in the throat.

2 hot dogs These are especially dangerous when cut into circular pieces. If serving hot dogs to young children, cut them lengthwise and then slice. As an extra precaution, cut the skin off.

3 raw fruits and vegetables Once your child has enough teeth to manage them, cut all uncooked fruits and veggies into thin strips. Cut carrots lengthwise rather than into circles. Don't serve raw peas, which can be inhaled. Celery should be sliced, not served in strips, because it's too stringy for young kids to swallow easily. Dice apples and pears, rather than cutting them into bite-size pieces.

4 peanuts and other tree nuts Nuts remain a choking hazard through about age seven and should not be served to young children.

5 hard candies

6 popcorn

7 seeds Kids can choke on snacks such as pumpkin or sunflower seeds. Also remove the seeds from watermelon and other fruits with seeds.

8 chewing gum

toddler snacks and meals

in addition to the family fare your toddler is learning to enjoy, try these menu items to boost your child's nutritional intake:

1 fruits and veggies with dips Dipping into a small cup of yogurt can add to the adventure of eating cut-up fruits and vegetables.

2 grated vegetables Grate zucchini, carrots, and other vegetables into soups, casseroles, and even muffin mixes.

3 english muffin pizzas In the broiler or oven, melt a tablespoon of tomato sauce and grated cheese over an English muffin.

4 mozzarella sticks These are fun and less fatty than American cheese.

5 flavored seltzer To cut down on overly sweet fruit juice and instead of soda, try flavored seltzers.

6 ice pops or frozen fruit bars These make a good substitute for fatty ice cream.

7 rice and beans This combo is high in protein and is an especially good choice for kids who don't like meat.

8 chicken nuggets Serve them home-broiled with olive oil.

foods to avoid or limit

Some foods have little or no place in a nutritious diet:

1 fake fat Sold under brand names such as Olestra, this artificial fat is used in some snack foods such as crackers and potato chips. This additive blocks the absorption of essential vitamins and may cause gastrointestinal cramping and diarrhea.

2 artificial sweeteners Any foods labeled "diet" contain sweeteners such as aspartame, which are not recommended for kids.

3 caffeine This drug affects kids in much the same way that it does adults, causing agitation, stomach upset, and difficulty sleeping. While few parents offer coffee to their toddlers, many are unaware of the high caffeine content of many kid-pleasing foods and beverages. A 12-ounce can of cola, for instance, contains 46 milligrams of caffeine, 12 ounces of Mountain Dew contains 54 milligrams, and an 8-ounce chocolate bar contains 22 milligrams (a cup of coffee contains about 100 milligrams). Children under age five should avoid caffeine as much as possible. Up through about age nine, kids should be limited to 50 milligrams or less per day.

4 sugar It's not necessary to eliminate refined sugar from your child's diet, but limiting high-sugar-content foods is a good choice. To satisfy your child's sweet tooth, offer fruits, which have vitamins and provide needed fiber.

5 refined grains Opt for whole grains over white-flour varieties when serving such foods as breads, pasta, and rice.

sleeping

getting enough sleep is essential to your child's physical and emotional health. In general, a one-year-old
needs about 14 hours of sleep a day, including nighttime
sleep and daytime naps. That need drops to 13 hours by
18 months, and as little as 11 or 12 by the time your child
is three. To ensure that your child gets the sleep he needs:

1 establish a bedtime routine Following a set
order of evening rituals—bathing, tooth brushing,
reading a book—helps a child learn to let go of the
day's activity.

2 adjust the daytime schedule If your child has
difficulty falling asleep at bedtime, shorten his afternoon nap. If he needs to stay up late so that he can
spend more time with you after work, lengthen his
afternoon nap. If your present work schedule prevents
you from seeing your child until late evening, consider
taking some work home to do after you've had some
time with him. You can also help your child readjust
his natural clock to the needs of your household.
Gradually over time, keep your early riser up a bit
later each night so he can adjust to sleeping later. Put
your night owl to bed a few minutes earlier each night.

3 avoid getting into bad habits To help your child
learn to put himself to sleep rather than rely on you,
always put him into his crib while he's still awake.
After the newborn stage, don't respond to every whim-
per or cry. If you know that your baby is not hungry,
give him the opportunity to soothe himself back to
sleep before going into his room. If you do go into his
room, refrain from picking him up. Keeping the lights
dim, gently rub his back and talk with him. Remind
him that it's time to sleep and leave the room again. If
he continues to cry, wait five minutes before returning
to him. Continue to reassure him with soft words, but
don't engage him in activity. Next time wait ten minutes,
and so on. Eventually, he will get the idea that it's his
job to sleep through the night.

sleep safety

o prevent accidents and to reduce the risk of sudden
infant death syndrome (SIDS) in babies:

1 ensure a safe sleep environment To review
safety measures and childproofing for your child's crib
and bedroom, see pages 49–52.

2 always place your baby on her back Until
your baby can easily roll over by herself, put her to
sleep on her back to reduce the risk of SIDS. Before
she can roll over, placing your baby on her tummy to
sleep can cause her to suffocate.

3 don't put your baby to bed with a bottle Milk
or juice can pool around her teeth, causing cavities in
baby teeth, which will affect not just these teeth, but
the condition of adult teeth, too.

4 turn out the lights Sleeping in a lit room reduces
the quality of sleep.

5 monitor the room temperature Your child will
awaken if she's too warm or cold. Babies over eight
pounds can regulate their body temperatures readily,
so it's unnecessary to keep a room warmer for your
child than is comfortable for you. In warmer weather,
use an air conditioner, but be sure that it doesn't blow
directly onto your child.

great bedtime books

Listening to a story is a time-honored part of the bedtime ritual. You'll want to save rollicking adventure stories and interactive books for other reading times. For bedtime, soothing rhymes and stories with themes about sleep are good choices. Particularly appealing bedtime stories for babies and infants include:

1 **Goodnight Moon** by Margaret Wise Brown (Also available in Spanish) (Harper & Row).

2 **Time for Bed** by Mem Fox (Harcourt Brace).

3 **Bedtime for Frances** by Russell Hoban (HarperCollins).

4 **Dr. Seuss' Sleep Book** by Dr. Seuss (Random House).

5 **And If the Moon Could Talk** by Kate Banks (Farrar, Straus & Giroux).

6 **Tell Me Something Happy Before I Go to Sleep** by Joyce Dunbar (Harcourt Brace).

7 **Papa, Please Get the Moon for Me** by Eric Carle (Little Simon).

8 **The Going to Bed Book** by Sandra Boynton (Little Simon).

9 **Good Night, Blue** by Angela Santomero (Simon Spotlight).

10 **How Many Kisses Good Night** by Jean Monrad, et. al (Random House).

11 **Hush Little Baby** by Sylvia Long (Chronicle Books).

clothing and dressing concerns

layette essentials

While it's tempting to overstock on all the cute little items made for newborns, keep in mind that infants grow quickly. The only things you really need to outfit your baby are:

- 8 to 10 **side-snap undershirts**
- 3 **onesies** (snap-crotch tee shirts, or bodysuits)
- 4 to 6 **sleeping gowns or kimonos**
- 2 to 3 **blanket sleepers**
- 4 to 6 **overalls** with feet
- 1 or 2 **sun hats or cool-weather hats**
- 3 pairs of **socks or booties**
- 3 washable **bibs**
- 2 to 3 **receiving blankets**
- 1 to 2 **sweaters**
- 1 **snowsuit** for cold-weather climates
- 1 special **dress-up outfit**

smart dressing

to ensure your baby's comfort and safety and to make the task of dressing your child easier for you:

1 look for easy-on, easy-off styles In over-the-head styles, look for wide necks or snaps at the neck, since babies dislike having clothing forced over their heads. Also look for styles that close in the front.

2 choose comfortable, well-fitting styles Clothing that is too large can snag on strollers or other items and presents both a tripping hazard when your child begins to toddle and a fire hazard near any open flame. Too-small clothing confines your baby's movements and is difficult to put on and take off.

3 opt for breathable fabrics Look for oversewn seams. Scratchy seams can irritate your child's skin. Many synthetic fibers don't breathe and can make your baby unpleasantly warm as well as contribute to diaper rash. Remove stiff labels.

4 avoid ornamentation Remove any decoration that your baby could chew off and swallow, or get tangled in, such as strings on hoods. Regularly check buttons and snaps to make sure that they are secure. Also check for loose strings that could wrap around your baby's fingers or toes.

5 skip the shoes Non-walkers don't need shoes. Footed garments can keep your baby's feet warm without feeling tight or restricting his movement.

first shoes

the best way to learn to walk is indoors in bare feet. Socks may be too slippery, and shoes inhibit the movement of your baby's feet and prevent his ability to grasp the floor's surface. But, once your baby is ready to take some steps outdoors, shoes are a must. When choosing shoes:

1 opt for a smooth sole Soles that grip the floor can trip a new walker.

2 choose a flexible style Canvas is a good choice since it allows your child's feet to breathe and bends with his movements.

3 go for low tops To promote ankle development.

4 get a good fit Buy shoes with a bit of growing room. The toe area should be large enough for your baby's foot to move easily, but not so large that it will trip him.

clothing hazards

be sure to avoid:

1 hoods, scarves, and neck pulls They can suffocate or strangle your child. When dressing your baby in winter, opt for a separate hat.

2 pom-poms and other decorations Remove any decorations that your infant can chew off and make sure that all buttons and other add-ons are securely sewn on for older kids.

3 zippers in boys' pants Until the preschool years, avoid pants with zippers for boys, who can, especially during the toilet-teaching stage, harm their penises with metal zippers.

4 ill-fitting clothing Clothing that's too large can be a fire hazard, snag on play equipment or furniture, or trip a child.

saving on clothing costs

clothing doesn't have to take a big bite out of your family's budget. To help keep costs down:

1 organize or join a clothing swap Join other local parents to recycle gently used items.

2 buy coordinated clothing When much of your child's clothing can be easily mixed and matched, you'll get more mileage out of each item your child has.

3 visit yard sales and consignment shops
Nearly new children's clothes can often be found at yard sales and used-clothing shops especially for kids.

4 hold on to ruined clothes for messy play
Instead of tossing an outfit that's hopelessly stained, save it for finger-painting.

5 find end-of-season sales While it can be a bit risky to anticipate, for instance, what size bathing suit your child will need next summer, any good guesses can give you enormous savings at season's end.

helping your child dress herself

your child feels a wonderful sense of competence when she learns to dress herself. To help make the process easier:

1 buy coordinating clothes For the clothes your child can choose from, go for a wardrobe with compatible tops and bottoms.

2 store complete outfits together Fold pants, shirts, and socks together so your child can grab a complete outfit that you've matched ahead of time.

3 buy only one color and style of socks This helps ensure that your child will make a match.

4 opt for easy-on-and-off styles This is especially important during the potty teaching phase. This includes shirts and sweaters with large neck bands, elastic-waisted pants and skirts, and tube socks rather than those with a designed heel section. Avoid clothing with buttons or zippers, except, of course, for coats.

5 pick clothes with an obvious front and back Or pick a style where it doesn't matter. Pocket tees or those with pictures instead of plain fronts make telling back from front easier. You can also teach your child to be on the lookout for labels, which tend to go in the back.

6 go for a good fit Sleeves or pant legs that have to be rolled up are not good choices for self-dressers. Likewise, items that have to be squeezed into make getting dressed harder and are uncomfortable to wear.

bathing, grooming, and toileting routines

bath essentials for the newborn

having the right equipment on hand can make giving your newborn a bath a safe and pleasant experience:

1 an unbreakable bowl Before your baby is ready for an immersion bath, you'll need a bowl that holds 12 to 16 ounces of water, or a well-scrubbed and well-rinsed sink.

2 cotton balls, swabs, and two soft washcloths You'll use some cotton balls to wash your baby's face around his eyes and others to wash his genital area. The swabs are handy for cleaning your baby's outer ear. One washcloth is for soaping your baby and the other for gentle rinsing.

3 soaps and shampoos Opt for products that are specially made for babies since these are gentler on tender skin.

4 two soft, absorbent towels Use one to hold him while you wash him and another to dry him off. For drying, use a hooded towel to prevent chills.

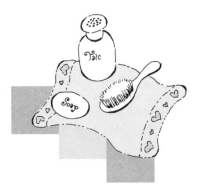

5 a nonskid rug It's important that the surface on which you're standing be safe and unlikely to cause slips.

6 a bath thermometer Available at most drug stores, a bath thermometer can help ensure that you keep the bathwater about the same as your baby's body temperature—between 90 and 100 degrees F.

giving your newborn a bath

to give your newborn a sponge bath:

1 fill a sink or small bowl with tepid tap water

2 undress and then wrap your baby in a towel

3 wash her eyes with a damp cotton ball Start at the bridge of her nose and work outward. Use a new cotton ball for each eye.

4 wash her face with a damp cloth There's no need to use soap on your newborn's face.

5 wash her neck and scalp You may use a gentle soap, although it's not necessary. If you do lather her up, use another damp cloth to rinse.

6 wash her chest, arms, and legs Be careful to avoid the umbilical stump.

7 wash her back Place your baby on her tummy.

8 wash her bottom and genitals last Use soap and clean carefully in the folds of your baby's skin. If your son has not been circumcised, do not attempt to retract the foreskin.

9 do not use any lotions, ointments, or talc

10 completely pat your baby dry and dress her

bathing your toddler

o help make your baby's bath both fun and safe, have these supplies on hand:

1 a nonskid bath mat or a baby bathtub Wherever you bathe your baby, be sure that the surface is nonskid. If you use the kitchen sink, be sure to turn the faucets away from your baby before placing him in the water. If you use the family tub, drape a towel over the edge to prevent injuries that could occur if he slips. If you use a separate baby bath, place it on a sturdy surface. Be sure to stand or kneel on a nonskid bath rug yourself during your baby's bath, since splashing is likely to result in water on the floor, which could lead to slips. Don't use bath seats: a baby or toddler can slip through and become trapped under the water.

2 faucet cover and knob covers These prevent your child from accidentally brushing against a hot surface or turning on the water.

3 child-strength soaps and shampoos If your child is at the stage when everything goes into his mouth, use liquid soap rather than bars. Choose unscented, nondeodorant soap and use it only on your child's hands, feet, and genital area. Soap of any kind, particularly on the face, will dry your child's tender skin.

4 soft washcloths or washcloth puppets If your child likes to chew everything, let him use washcloths and puppets before you've lathered him. Avoid sponges, which young children can bite into, creating a choking hazard.

5 a shampoo guard If your child hates having his hair rinsed after a shampoo, consider investing in a shampoo guard, which sits like a halo around your child's forehead and directs soapy water away from his face.

6 bath toys Specially designed toys suitable for submersion such as floating ducks and boats, books, pails, plastic cups, and colanders prod your child's scientific experimentation.

bathtime activities

in addition to providing toys that your child can enjoy in the bath, try these activities:

1 eat messy foods The bath is the perfect place to enjoy a drippy ice pop, and cleanup—of both your child and the tub—is simple.

2 draw on your child's creativity Nontoxic water paints and specially designed bath paints can bring out the artist in your young bather.

3 experiment Pose some interesting questions to your toddler and let her experiment to find the answers. For instance, show your child a rubber ball and a spoon and ask, "Which one will float?" Or ask, "What will happen if you pour the water from the pail into the cup?"

4 blow bubbles Use store-bought or homemade bubbles and wands to create a bubble-filled room. Or fill a paper or plastic cup with plain water and let your child use a straw to create a watery froth.

5 bathe a doll Let your child take a bath-safe doll into the tub so she can practice playing the grown-up.

hair-care ideas

Whether your child has a few wisps or a curly head-ful of hair, caring for it requires some expertise. For starters:

1 go easy on shampoo Before the age of three months or so, unless your child has sweated heavily or otherwise gotten his hair dirty, shampoo is unnecessary. When you do use shampoo, choose a baby-safe variety and use only a bit.

2 don't overwash In hot weather, your child may need a daily wash, but most of the time, every other day or even twice a week is sufficient.

3 rinse thoroughly Soap attracts dirt and any residue will make hair dirty faster. Under-rinsed hair can also cause itching and flaking. Experiment with ways to ease your child's fear of getting soap in her eyes while rinsing. A shampoo guard may do the trick; you could encourage her to hold her head far back during rinsing by putting pictures on the ceiling; or try letting your child do it herself.

4 avoid tangles A careful combing with a blunt-tipped, wide-toothed comb after rinsing will remove most tangles. Cream rinses and spray-in detanglers can help unsnarl long hair, but they aren't necessary for most children. If your child has long hair, consider braiding it loosely before bedtime to avoid nighttime tangling. Letting your child sleep on a satin pillow-case—once she's over the age of two, when it's safe to let your child sleep with a firm pillow—can also cut down on tangles.

5 get a good cut Stylists who are experienced at working with children are a good bet for your child's professional haircutting. Blunt cuts are less prone to tangling.

6 don't overstyle or decorate Tightly made braids can damage the roots and cause hair loss. Rubber bands can cause split ends, a major cause of tangling. Opt for coated bands when braiding your child's hair or putting it in a ponytail. Avoid putting any decorations in your young child's hair, since they can slip off and present a choking hazard. Stretchy hair bands can give your child a headache.

mini manicures

irty fingernails are perfect breeding grounds for germs, so it's a good idea to keep your child's nails trimmed short. Here are some pointers to keep in mind:

1 use a soft-bristle toothbrush or nail brush Wash under your child's nails. Warm soap and water and a gentle scrubbing also make your child's nail more pliable and easier to trim.

2 use blunt-tip safety scissors or nail clippers

3 trim nails just to the tip of the finger If you trim too low you risk cutting your child and encouraging ingrown nails, a painful condition.

4 use a soft emery board to smooth rough edges Between and after trimming, smooth edges to help keep your child from biting and pulling on his nails.

5 consider trimming during sleep Babies squirm and toddlers are notorious for not wanting to see any part of themselves cut away, including their fingernails. If your child has any qualms about having his nails trimmed, wait until he's asleep to do it.

caring for your baby's teeth

t he care of your child's baby teeth can ensure a lifetime of good oral health. Here are some tooth-care facts to brush up on:

1 get annual dental checkups The American Academy of Pediatric Dentistry recommends that a child have his first dental appointment by 18 months of age at the latest, and ideally, within six months after the arrival of the first tooth. After that, yearly dental visits are recommended.

2 begin brushing early Even before teeth have erupted, you can aid your child's oral health by gently washing his gums with a dampened piece of gauze. When teeth do come in, get a soft- or medium-bristle toothbrush and gently brush with plain water. By age two, you can begin teaching your child to brush his own teeth, but you'll have to supervise the procedure for a few years to come.

3 begin flossing early, too Most kids can't learn to floss on their own until they're six or so, but parents can do the job for younger kids. It's especially useful for kids who have closely spaced teeth for which brushing alone can't remove impacted food particles.

4 less is more when it comes to toothpaste

Overuse of fluoride toothpaste can stain your child's teeth. Use just enough to cover half the bristle-area of the brush.

5 brush right

Have your child brush up and down and back and forth for at least two minutes a day. His dentist can show you the preferred method.

6 zero in on the most important brushing

While brushing morning, night, and after meals and snacks is ideal, if your child can't brush that often, just be sure he brushes at night, because removing food particles before bed will greatly reduce the buildup of plaque-causing bacteria during sleep.

7 find brushing substitutes

Eating cheddar cheese can reduce oral bacteria, so follow up meals and snacks with a piece of cheddar for kids who are old enough to chew it safely. Also, get your child in the habit of drinking water after snacks and meals to help wash away food particles.

8 don't overdo — or underdo — fluoride

If your water supply is fluoridated and your child drinks at least 12 ounces of tap water a day, there's no need for additional fluoride treatments. Too much fluoride ingestion in young children can cause permanent teeth to come in with mottled stains. However, if your water supply is not fluoridated or if your child drinks bottled water, fluoride treatments can be beneficial. Check with your dentist or pediatrician.

9 watch the diet

Foods rich in calcium and vitamins D and C are essential for building strong teeth. Foods heavy in sugar and starch, including fruit juices, are prime triggers of plaque buildup and cavities.

time to begin toilet-teaching

learning to use the toilet is a major event for both toddlers and their parents. The process is gradual and usually begins sometime between the ages of 18 months and three years. Exactly when your child is ready depends on both physical and psychological factors. These cues from your child indicate that the time to begin teaching has arrived:

1 nighttime dryness If your child regularly wakes up in the morning with a dry diaper, doesn't urinate during naps, and goes for longer dry periods during the day, you know that her bladder has grown enough to allow her some control.

2 predictable bowel habits Having BMs on a fairly regular schedule, such as every morning after breakfast, helps enable your child to predict her need for the toilet.

3 ability to self-dress Your child's ability to pull her pants up and down is essential in the toilet-teaching process.

4 discomfort when wet or soiled Your child's ability to recognize that her diapers need changing because the wetness or BM is uncomfortable is a major signal that she's ready for toilet-teaching.

5 ability to follow directions

6 understanding of related words Your child should understand words that apply to toilet-teaching, such as "wet" and "potty."

7 an understanding of what the toilet is for

steps to toilet-teaching

O nce your child has indicated a readiness to begin toilet-teaching, choose a relatively stress-free time in his life—not when he's about to begin preschool or around the time that a new sibling has joined the family. It's also helpful to begin daytime training during warmer months when your child won't be wearing layers of heavy clothing. Stock up on underpants—these can be a great motivator. Then take a step-by-step approach:

1 help your child recognize his bodily functions
First decide what words you want your child to use for bathroom functions. When you notice that he's urinating or defecating, say, "You're making BMs in your diaper" or "Do you feel your diaper becoming warm and wet? That's because you're urinating."

2 introduce him to the potty or child seat
Let him know its purpose. Encourage him to sit on it, fully clothed at first, and to introduce it to his dolls and stuffed animals.

3 begin to schedule regular potty times
Try for times when he's likely to have to urinate or defecate, but don't insist that he make his deposit into the potty or toilet. If he initially chooses to sit on the potty while wearing his diaper, let him do it, which provides practice in urinating or defecating while sitting down. As he gets more used to sitting on the potty or toilet, begin to schedule a session every two hours or so.

4 arrange a signal
He can use this to tell you he has to use the potty.

5 don't overpraise success
Nor should you show disappointment for "failures." Your child's motivation needs to be his own comfort and sense of accomplishment, not your feelings.

6 expect accidents
Simply let him know that he should be proud of his accomplishments and reassure him that he can try to use the toilet or potty next time.

discipline

dealing with dawdling

Children operate on a different clock than adults and do not recognize the need to speed up when time grows short. To reduce the stress caused by your toddler's dawdling and inattentiveness:

1 identify dawdling moments Determine when your need to hurry conflicts with your child's need to take her time, and try to adjust your schedule. If you find, for instance, that getting yourself out to work and your child to day care frequently leads to frustration, build additional time into your schedule to allow for the predictable delays.

2 give your child transition time Refocusing attention from one activity to another can be very difficult for some children. Give your child a warning that she needs to redirect her attention a few minutes earlier. You might put on familiar music and say something like, "When this song ends, we need to put on our coats and head outside."

3 maintain rituals Following rituals helps your child make the necessary transition from one activity to the next and reduces the stress that arises from not knowing what comes next.

4 make a game of keeping up To hurry your child along when necessary, set a timer or wind up a music box and say, "Let's see if we can pick up all the toys before the buzzer goes off." Then join your child in a race to the finish.

5 make eye contact When your child appears to be ignoring your request to get moving, it is probably because she's engrossed in another activity and really can't focus on your words alone. Getting down on the floor with your child and looking directly at her helps her disengage from her activity and focus on you.

interrupting interruptions

your child wants your attention and he wants it now. While you certainly can't ask your infant to postpone her needs, you're right to begin teaching your toddler that he may, on occasion, have to wait for your full attention. To introduce the concept:

1 split your focus when you can For example, give your child a hug as you remind him to stay quiet while you're on the phone.

2 provide alternatives to your attention Set up other activities your child can perform near you. While you're busy paying the bills, he can sit across the table from you and color, or while you're on the phone, he can play with quiet toys.

3 make a date Because his sense of time is so limited, use something concrete, such as a kitchen timer or a familiar audio or video tape to mark the time at which you'll be available. Say, "I will be able to play with you when the tape ends." Be sure to keep your word. Then say, "Thank you for waiting. I'm ready now, just as I promised." Experiences such as these reinforce the notion that waiting has a payoff and that his needs will be fulfilled.

4 don't interrupt your child Show your child the same respect you're asking of him. When you're engaged in conversation or a project with him, don't abandon him simply because another adult enters the room. Be obvious with your desire to continue your time with him, saying to the other adult, perhaps, "I'll be with you in a minute. Right now, Jack is telling me a story about his visit to the zoo."

winning over whining

j ust as your infant learned to coo to get your attention, your toddler practices a number of different voices to see what works with you. Whining takes hold when your child learns that it gets your attention. To reduce whining:

1 identify the problem Sometimes, whining is the result of being tired or hungry. If that's the case, ignore the whining and correct the underlying problem. Other times, legitimate complaints are presented in a whining voice. When responding to a problem presented in a whine, acknowledge the problem and include a reminder not to whine. "I know you're angry that you can't play in the rain, but I like to hear you talk in your regular voice."

2 state your policy on whining clearly When your child whines as a way of asking for something, simply say, "I don't listen to whining. Ask in your good voice." It's not necessary to give in to every request, even when stated in the proper voice, however. Respond to the request in a legitimate way, giving in—or not— depending on what you feel is the right choice.

3 use humor You might pretend to capture the whine in your hands and throw it away. Or, in a playful manner, you could whine back. Just be sure your child knows that you're not making fun of her.

4 ignore it If the above ideas don't work, ignore the whining. Avoid making eye contact and keep your manner and expression neutral, even if you're angry.

5 have a time out If whining escalates, tell your child that she'll have to go to another room, or, if you're out, that you'll have to take her home. Follow through.

6 offer praise When the whining stops, praise your child and thank her for speaking correctly.

how to respond to aggressive behavior

toddlers, with their limited vocabularies, often resort to clearly unacceptable behaviors to express their point. These are not behaviors that you can ignore, but overreacting could cause more harm than good. If another child has taken away his toy, for instance, your child may respond automatically by grabbing back the toy and pushing his friend away. A gentle reminder and a recognition of what caused his behavior may be all that is needed to prevent further aggression. If, on the other hand, your child seems intent on harming another, shows a regular pattern of aggression, or takes pleasure in harming others, you need to intervene with the help of a trained professional so that your child learns early on to curb his aggression. Here's how to deal with the ordinary crimes and misdemeanors that toddlers are more likely to commit:

1 acknowledge your child's action Intervene immediately when you have witnessed your child acting aggressively toward another. Separate him from the child he has hurt. If you're the subject of his aggression, hold him firmly away from you at arm's length to prevent him from repeating the action.

2 recognize your child's motivation While aggression is not acceptable, toddlers usually have good cause (to them) for biting, hitting, or pinching. Inform your child you're aware of what's behind his actions, by saying something such as, "I know you don't like it when your friend takes away your toy."

3 state the rules clearly Follow up your acknowledgment of his motivation with a clear statement of the rules. "Even though you're angry, you are not allowed to hit."

4 encourage your child to use words Help your child put his feelings and his needs into words by teaching him to say, "Don't take my toy." Encourage both children to discuss their feelings. Point out how hurtful it is to have a toy taken away and how hurtful it is to be hit.

5 encourage him to seek an adult's help During the toddler years, don't expect your child to work out his problems with a playmate on his own. Teach him to seek out you or another grown-up if he feels he's being wronged rather than to lash out physically against his friend.

6 teach your child to say, "I'm sorry" By age two, most kids can apologize for a misbehavior.

7 don't respond in kind Hitting a child for hitting or biting him back is counterproductive.

toddler cursing: words to the wise

as they learn the power of language, some toddlers use words they know are naughty to get attention. If your child blurts out words that would shock a sailor:

1 don't laugh It may seem funny at first to hear such language fall from the lips of your babe, but letting her know that only encourages more of the same. Don't quote your child to another adult for a laugh either, at least not within your child's hearing.

2 don't overreact Acting shocked or horrified teaches that the word is powerful, thus giving your child incentive to repeat it.

3 ignore the first incident It's possible that your child has no idea that she's uttered an inappropriate word and may simply be repeating a new word much as she would any other new word. Paying no attention to the word can help it disappear from her vocabulary.

4 remind your child of the rules If your child repeats a forbidden word, state firmly, "We don't use that word in our family."

5 set a good example If you curse or swear, expect your child to do the same. Modeling appropriate verbal responses to anger helps your child learn socially acceptable language, too.

taming tantrums

during the toddler years, your child is constantly learning to control his impulses, his bodily functions, and his behavior. Sometimes, the ability to maintain self-control breaks down, resulting in a tantrum. You may not be able to avoid them entirely, but you can minimize their frequency and intensity. To tame your child's outbursts:

1 practice prevention Making sure your child is well-rested and not unduly stressed can prevent many tantrums.

2 loosen the reins a bit Make sure your toddler has freedom and time to run and play without worrying about making a mess or being stopped from engaging in fun activities. Save your "nos" for really important issues.

3 stay calm When your child does have a tantrum, he needs you to remain in control. Try gently, but firmly, holding your child to keep him from hurting himself or others. Move him away from the source of his anger and give him a chance to recover.

4 distract him Before a tantrum reaches full throttle, your child may be responsive to a change in scenery or other distraction.

5 try humor For a mild tantrum, try defusing the situation with humor. Just be careful that your child knows you're not making fun of him.

6 help undo frustration If your toddler is frustrated because he can't, say, put on his shoes, help him master that art so that he can feel a sense of accomplishment instead. In cases of safety, acknowledge

your child's desire to, for example, climb a ladder, but restate your rule firmly: "I know you want to climb up high, but that's not allowed." Offer an alternative, if possible: "Later we can go to the park and you can climb the slide ladder."

7 don't give in to demands Public tantrums cause some parents to give in simply to reduce embarrassment, but this response will only serve to ensure that your child will repeat the tantrum the next time you're out. Ignore what others may say or think in such cases, and focus on your child. As calmly as possible, state your rule and get on with business: "You will not get what you want by crying and kicking. When you calm down, we can talk about it."

8 take a time-out if needed If you're afraid of losing control with your child, turn your back and count to ten, once you're sure that he cannot harm himself or someone else. Don't walk out, which could terrify a child who is already feeling out of control. Simply say, "I'm getting very angry and I have to turn away for a moment until I'm calmer."

9 discuss the tantrum After your child has calmed down, talk about what made him so upset. Don't dwell on the outburst, however. Instead, assure him of your love with a warm hug, and join him in a pleasant activity.

10 don't take your child's behavior personally Don't allow yourself to feel guilty or out of control because your child has had a momentary breakdown. Though having your child shout "I hate you" can be hurtful, it's important to keep in mind that your child's actions are not so much directed at you as they are simply a show of his own frustrations.

encouraging cooperation

more important than correcting misbehaviors is encouraging the behavior you want. To help your child become cooperative:

1 notice desired behavior Catch your child in the act of being good. Note when she shares a toy, saying, "That was nice how you let your friend push your doll carriage." Or, "Thank you for helping to pick up your toys." The good feeling she gets from your verbal reward makes it more likely that she'll strive to repeat the behavior.

2 offer preemptory compliments Anticipate occasions for which your child might forget the rules, and jump in with an early "thank you." For instance, if your child has not interrupted you for 20 seconds into a phone call, say, "Thank you for letting me talk," before she has a chance to interrupt. She'll feel good about her behavior and seek to garner further approval.

3 don't bribe Nonmaterial rewards help your child focus on cooperating. Offering your child a bribe, however, such as "I'll buy you a candy if you're good at the store," sets your child and you up for ever-escalating demands for payment in return for the desired behavior. A better response would be, "Because you were so well behaved in the store, I got my shopping done quickly. Now I have time for a trip to the park with you."

4 follow rituals and routines When your child expects dinner to be followed by bath, followed by a story before bed, she is far less likely to negotiate at every turn.

honing your child's decision-making skills

Within the framework of your family's routines, your child needs to practice making decisions on his own. To help him hone his skills:

1 don't overwhelm with too many choices Give your child limited options, such as whether to wear his blue or his green sweater.

2 don't offer choices that you can't live with Refrain from asking what your child wants to wear, for instance, if you're not willing to let him go to day care in a polka-dotted shirt and striped shorts in the winter.

3 let your child experience natural consequences Within the bounds of safety and common sense, let your child practice making decisions, even bad ones. For instance, if your child wants to drop an old book or magazine into his wading pool, you can allow him to learn on his own that the paper will be ruined by his action.

4 don't overreact to mistakes Making mistakes is a valuable part of learning. When your child makes a wrong decision, give him the opportunity to learn from it. Don't admonish harshly, for instance, if he uses a crayon to draw on the walls. Say, "Crayons are for paper only. I will put the crayons away for a while because you used them on the wall." Then have your child help you clean up the mess in a matter-of-fact way.

5 make appropriate decisions Your child needs you to decide for him in matters of health, safety, and learning right from wrong. Don't leave it up to him to determine if he needs to wear a hat on a freezing-cold day or hold your hand in a crowded parking lot. Simply state the rules without offering alternatives.

say please and thank you

teaching manners is a fundamental way to teach your child values—that is, to value the needs of others. Begin with small steps that will appeal to your child's self-interest. For instance, let her know that people will like her better if she shows consideration to others. Stress that good manners are not merely a list of dos and don'ts, but a way to help other people feel good. These practices will make instilling manners easier:

1 model the behavior you want Your child learns more about manners by observing your behavior toward others than by following your verbal instructions.

2 be realistic in your goals Like all teaching, you need to tailor your expectations to your child's level of development. You can't expect a two-year-old to sit politely in a fancy restaurant, so for the sake of others, it's best to avoid such social situations until your child is ready for them. On the other hand, you can expect your toddler to learn to say "please" and "thank you" and not to screech her dismay when you stop to talk to a neighbor for a moment.

3 don't get involved in power plays While teaching the rules of civilized behavior, don't insist that your child say the "magic words" each and every time she makes a request. Just offer reminders, such as "I like it better when you say please when you ask for something."

4 prepare ahead of time By the time your child approaches age three, she's able to retain information for long periods and is able to control some of her impulses. Use these newfound skills to rehearse potentially unmannerly episodes beforehand. For instance, before attending a birthday party, remind your child that it's her friend's turn to open the presents.

5 keep criticism to a minimum Reminders rather than demands work best. For example, say, "Remember to keep your mouth closed while you're chewing," instead of scolding.

6 make manners fun Have a pretend tea party and practice being ever-so-polite. Engage your child in behaviors such as writing thank-you notes by having her add her own drawing to your note.

playtime
fun and
learning

reading and language skills

great books for your baby

It's never too soon to introduce your child to the wonder of books. These classics will help your child develop a lifelong love of reading:

1 I Am a Baby! by Elizabeth Hathon (McClanahan Book Co).

2 What Do Babies Do? by Debby Slier (Random House).

3 "More, More, More" Said the Baby by Vera Williams (Tupelo Books).

4 Spot's Toys by Eric Hill (Putnam).

5 Tana Hoban's What Is It? by Tana Hoban (Tupelo Books).

6 Finger Rhymes by Marc Tolon Brown (Puffin).

7 Black on White by Tana Hoban (Greenwillow).

8 Tickle, Tickle by Helen Oxenbury (Simon & Schuster).

9 From Head to Toe by Eric Carle (HarperCollins).

10 Richard Scarry's Best First Book Ever by Richard Scarry (Random House).

11 Baby! Talk! by Penny Gentieu (Crown).

12 Pat the Bunny by Dorothy Kunhardt (Golden).

great books for your toddler

These classic books make a valuable addition to your child's library:

1 The Tale of Peter Rabbit by Beatrix Potter (Little Simon). This classic, first issued in 1902, helps kids deal with their desire for independence while still wanting to stay close to home.

2 Curious George by H. A. Rey (Houghton Mifflin). George's talent is getting himself in and out of trouble, a trait young children can easily identify with.

3 The Runaway Bunny by Margaret Wise Brown (HarperCollins). The theme of independence and need is beautifully explored in this classic by the author of *Goodnight Moon*.

4 Mike Mulligan and His Steam Shovel by Virginia Lee Burton (Houghton Mifflin). Like the steam shovel, young readers will see themselves as small but powerful.

5 Corduroy by Don Freeman (Viking). The importance of friendship and acceptance will reassure children who are just learning about making friends.

6 The Carrot Seed by Ruth Krauss (HarperCollins). Big plans and determination create an inspiring story of a boy and his garden.

7 Swimmy by Leo Lionni (Knopf). A problem-solving little fish makes the underwater world a safer place for small creatures like himself.

8 The Very Hungry Caterpillar by Eric Carle (Putnam). Kids love watching and listening as a caterpillar eats its way through this book.

9 Harold and the Purple Crayon by Crockett Johnson (HarperCollins). When his imagination joins a purple crayon, Harold builds a world of wonder.

10 Tomie de Paola's Mother Goose Favorites (Grosset & Dunlap). Paola's art may be familiar to young readers and the rhymes are a treasure to share.

ways to make reading a part of every day

In addition to making it a part of soothing bedtime rituals, there are many opportunities to engage your child in reading throughout the day. Try these for starters:

1 carry books wherever you go Keep a stock of small books in your bag to read to your child whenever the mood strikes, such as in the playground or while waiting in line in the grocery store.

2 take turns reading Encourage your child to "read" to you by retelling a favorite story or by making up a story to go with pictures.

3 share old magazines Give your child supervised access to old magazines, particularly ones with pictures of children. Your child will delight in turning—and tearing—the pages.

4 interact with books By age ten months or so, your baby knows enough words to respond to books in a whole new way. When looking at a picture book together, ask your child to point out items on a page.

5 teach an important word The first word that a child learns to recognize is her name. Write your child's name on her bedroom door, on her toy box, on her pillowcase. Each time she encounters it, ask, "What does that word say?" She'll soon delight in finding her name everywhere.

6 follow your child's lead Never insist on reading when your child is not interested, and try to find the time whenever she is.

7 respect your child's need for repetition Don't be surprised if your child insists that you read the same book over and over again. Repetition is an important part of learning and by hearing a favorite story repeated, your child truly makes it her own.

8 be dramatic Even if you'd never perform on stage, don't be shy about embellishing your reading with dramatic flair, adopting different voices for various characters, and acting out scenes with abandon.

9 ask questions Stop during a story and ask questions, such as "What happened?" or "What do you think will happen next?"

10 go for variety While your reading time may be made up mostly of picture and story books, alternate with poetry and some simple nonfiction now and then.

11 visit the library Attend story hours. Check out books for your child to enjoy at home. Ask the children's librarian to suggest books that will appeal to your child's special interests.

12 read the world Point out words in the outdoor environment such as "Stop" on a stop sign, or "drug store" or "supermarket." Help her find words that include the letters in her name if she's interested, but don't insist.

13 engage your child in practical reading experiences Let your child join you in following a recipe as you read it from a cookbook. Read cards that you receive in the mail aloud to your child. When writing a personal letter, invite your child to add her own scrawl at the bottom or have her hit a few keys as you send an e-mail.

14 model reading Let your child see you enjoying reading.

ready for reading

most kids aren't ready to begin decoding words on a page until sometime around age five to seven. But long before then, they can learn these prereading skills:

1 point to words as you read Lots of exposure to books and other reading material will help your child learn that the English language (and many others) is read from the top of the page to the bottom and from the left side to the right. As you read, follow along with your finger to help your child absorb this standard.

2 learn shapes Letters are made up of shapes. Long before your child can learn to recognize letters, he can learn all about simple shapes. On walks, point out squares, circles, and triangles around him. As he approaches age three, encourage him to draw various shapes and to find shapes in letters.

3 play listening games Help your child learn to recognize sounds in words. For example, read poetry with alliteration and rhyme. Sing songs. Play sound games such as naming all the things in the house that start with the same sound, and help your child discover the butter, (stuffed) bear, bib, and more around him.

4 talk Engage your child in frequent conversations and ask questions to help him learn the fundamentals of storytelling while enriching his vocabulary.

5 honor books Set up a special shelf for your child's books. Help him choose books to give as gifts at his friends' birthday parties. While many of his books should be nearly impossible-to-destroy board books, teach him to care for more fragile books in a special way.

6 don't push Children under the age of five or so should not be prodded to read. There's no need to invest in flash cards or computer games that purport to teach toddlers to decode. This kind of pressure to perform can undermine your child's confidence as well as his interest in reading.

building a library

h aving books to call her own goes a long way to helping your child learn to love books and reading. To create a home library for your child:

1 make books accessible Have a special shelf (untippable and not too high) just for your child. Or reserve a low shelf on the family bookcase for her collection alone.

2 scatter some books around the house In addition to a central place where most of her books are kept, keep books handy in every room. Store favorite bedtime tales near your child's bed. Keep a book or two on the coffee table, and have some handy in the car, too.

3 ask for gift books When a special occasion rolls around, ask that friends give books to your child so that her collection grows.

4 visit yard sales Purchase piles of used books for a fraction of their original cost. Libraries often have once-a-year sales to clear their shelves.

word power: building your child's vocabulary

a language-rich environment not only aids in your child's eventual reading skills, but helps him develop social and logic skills. To build your child's word power:

1 talk frequently From the moment you meet your newborn, talk to him. During infancy, encourage him to keep up her part of the conversation by responding to his coos and babbles. Introduce meaningful words. For instance, when you're placing a soft blanket on him, say "soft." Guide his hands over it and repeat "soft." He'll soon associate words with their meanings. As your child moves from babbles to words, continue to encourage conversation. Ask questions. Listen attentively to what your child has to say.

2 use precise words The more words your child hears, the more he'll learn. Instead of asking him to give you a toy, ask for "the tiny red car." On an outing to the zoo say, "See the lioness and her cubs" rather than "See the animals."

3 use synonyms While "big" or "small" may perfectly describe an object, substituting words such as "tremendous" or "tiny" expand your child's word bank in both enormous and minuscule ways.

4 make up words Not every word needs to have a place in Webster's. Have fun with your child giving silly names to common objects. For instance, a hat could be a "beanie topper" or even a "hootitooti." Read aloud Lewis Carroll's wonderful nonsense poem "Jabberwocky."

5 read Every new book is bound to include a new word or concept.

enhancing listening skills

earning to listen takes a long time to master, requiring an attention span that few toddlers have yet acquired. However, there are some things you can do to help your child improve her listening skills:

1 engage in lots of one-to-one conversation
While kids benefit simply from being exposed to the family chatter, making time to sit down and have a conversation between just the two of you (about anything at all) urges your child to concentrate on hearing what you have to say.

2 whisper A soft voice draws your child in and inspires her to focus on your words.

3 be brief Toddlers lose focus when you speak in long sentences or speak for too long without sufficient pausing.

4 make eye contact When you need your child to listen, get down on her level and look her directly in the eye.

5 ask for feedback When you need to know whether your child has heard you, ask her to repeat what you said.

6 play with rhymes Exposure to lots of nursery rhymes and songs helps your child differentiate between similar-sounding words.

7 use big words now and then Kids are drawn to the new and unusual. If your child has heard you say, "That's nice!" dozens of times, her ears will perk up when you state, "That's extraordinary!"

talk soup: what you should know about your child's speaking skills

most toddlers develop enough language skills to be understood by people outside the family by the time they're about three. If you suspect that your child's language development is delayed or his use of language is incorrect:

1 have a professional evaluation Your pediatrician can refer you to a local speech and language pathologist if your child's language skills are lagging. It's vital to get intervention early, since most problems can be rectified completely if caught in time.

2 don't overcorrect Don't worry if your child mispronounces words or uses nonstandard syntax now and then. Certain sounds, such as the letters "r" and "th" are nearly impossible for most toddlers to master. Misusing irregular words is a normal part of the learning process. Saying "foots" instead of "feet," for example, is a sign that your child is absorbing the usual rule of syntax that requires an "s" for plurals.

3 model the language you want When your child says something such as "He goed home," repeat his observations using correct syntax, saying, "Yes, he went home."

4 encourage, but don't insist on, speech Engage your child in verbal communication even if he prefers to point to the things he wants. If he's at a stage in which he could be more verbal, simply say, "I like it better when you use words instead of pointing," while handing him the object.

5 be patient with stuttering Many children pass through a stuttering stage of a few months when their ideas come faster than their ability to enunciate. If stuttering becomes chronic, consult with your child's pediatrician. In the meantime, be patient. Don't correct your child or show frustration.

6 check out lisping Lisping is an inability to correctly pronounce words that contain the "s" or "z" sounds. It can be the result of physical abnormalities of the mouth or teeth, a hearing difficulty, or simply mimicking another lisper. If a lisp persists for more than a few weeks, discuss the problem with your child's pediatrician.

social skills

planning playdates

C hildren under the age of two tend to play side by side, interacting with one another as they would interact with toys. Nevertheless, from infancy on, children benefit from exposure to other children, learning from them and simply enjoying the company of peers. From the age of two on, real interactions are possible. To help your child have happy playtimes:

1 plan ahead If the playdate is at your home, double-check all your childproofing, since your visitor might be drawn to objects that your child has already learned are off-limits.

2 have constant supervision Don't expect two lively toddlers to keep out of trouble for even a minute without adult supervision.

3 don't overmanage the playdate While you need to remain nearby, don't try to direct the play or inter-fere with minor squabbles if no one is getting hurt. Interceding too soon tells your child that you don't trust her to work out the details of her friendships on her own.

4 plan around nap and feeding schedules The best time for children to enjoy one another's company is when both are rested and well fed.

5 seek out neutral territory Many toddlers become territorial in their own homes and are able to interact better with their peers in neutral territory such as the local playground.

6 make sharing easier Try to have duplicates of some items so that children aren't drawn to the same plaything. For instance, if you're taking your child to the playground on her tricycle, suggest that her play-mate's parent also have a tricycle on hand. If your child has a special toy that she's not ready to share, put it away until after the playdate.

7 look for playmates with a similar temperament
Your boisterous toddler may have more fun with
another ready-to-go kid than she would with a quieter,
more subdued child. Likewise, your timid child may
feel overwhelmed by a more active playmate.

8 broaden the range of friendships From time to
time, set up playdates with older or younger children
to give your toddler the chance to learn from a bigger
kid or to teach a younger one.

9 evaluate what works and what doesn't After
a playdate, review what went well and what didn't so
you can plan accordingly for the next time.

games that teach social skills

through play, your child can learn to share, take turns,
and, in general, behave civilly toward others. These
games can help:

1 follow the leader You can engage a number of
toddlers in this game by naming and acting out a
variety of movements—the sillier, the better. For
added fun, set up a simple obstacle course, leading
kids in climbing over a pillow, crawling into a tunnel
made from an open box, and walking around a chair.

2 large-space coloring On a sidewalk with chalk,
or at home with a large piece of paper and crayons,
encourage two or more kids to draw together.

3 dance Put on some music, get into the act, and
watch your toddler and her friends dance up a storm.

4 ring-around-a-rosy This old-time favorite helps
your toddler learn teamwork as well as increase her
coordination.

teaching your toddler to share

Sharing is not easy for a toddler, who naturally thinks that the world belongs to him. To introduce your child to the fine art of sharing:

1 practice sharing A two-year-old doesn't believe that if he relinquishes an object it will come back to him, especially not from another child. He'll be more willing to share with you, whom he trusts, than with a playmate. Practice sharing with him, being obvious about what you're doing. Say, "I want to share my cookie with you." Then give him some. Next, offer him a whole cookie and say, "Now it's your turn to share your cookie with me." Practice at home will make sharing easier in other settings.

2 focus on the value of sharing Talk about the good feelings that come from sharing. Let him know that the more he is willing to share, the more others are likely to want to share with him.

3 explain that your child's possessions are his Tell your child explicitly that his toys belong to him even when another child plays with them, just as the other child's toys remain hers when she shares them.

4 have good sharing toys available Dress-up clothes, building blocks, and tea sets encourage children to interact with each other. Have enough pieces so that each child gets to play with some of them.

5 encourage side-by-side play Don't devote an entire playdate to sharing. Plan some activities, such as coloring, that children can do alongside one another, with each having his own book and crayon supply.

physical development

great baby games

even before his first birthday, your child can enjoy these rollicking games that help develop both his muscles and his budding sense of identity:

1 lap rides A moderate amount of movement from the safety of your lap is a real thrill for your baby, especially when accompanied by a nursery rhyme. Just be extremely careful not to let him fall or to jostle his head or neck.

2 peek-a-boo This favorite is never out of style with infants, and it is great for helping them understand that you are still there even when they can't see you.

3 where is it? Let your baby see you hide an object under a blanket and then ask, "Where is it?" As your baby becomes adept at finding a single object, help lengthen his attention span by hiding two or three objects.

4 patting and clapping games Rhymes that include action, such as "pat-a-cake" and "This little piggy ... " involve many of your child's senses, and as he becomes familiar with these games, he delights in anticipating your next move.

5 find your nose Your baby loves all of his many parts and pointing them out can be a real thrill. Ask, "Where is your nose?" "Where are your toes?" and watch your child thrill at his ability to point to the right place.

6 come and get it Place a toy or other appealing object just out of your child's reach and encourage him to grab for it or crawl toward it. Be sure to let him enjoy the sense of accomplishment that comes from reaching his target.

parents ALERT!

Never shake a baby or young child. Rough play and bouncing without cradling your child's neck and head can lead to serious injury, including mental retardation, blindness, and death. Be sure that you and anyone handling your infant knows how to hold him, always bracing his head and neck securely.

large muscle skills

most of your toddler's day is a whirl of physical activity. These activities will add to her fun, as well as hone her growing coordination:

1 climbing Now that crawling and walking are old hat, your child will relish opportunities to reach new heights. Now's the time to let her practice going up and down the stairs. Teach her to hold your hand or the banister on her way up and how to turn around safely to make her way down. Let her experiment to see if she prefers descending on her bottom or backwards, with her hands grasping the stair above.

2 tumbling Create soft, safe play spaces where your child can roll around, fall, and practice tumbling. Turn a room into a carnival for her simply by placing a mattress on the floor away from any sharp-edged furniture.

3 ball kicking While toddlers lack the coordination to pitch and catch smaller balls, kicking and chasing a huge beach ball for great distances is a thrill.

4 tagging Games of tag are great fun, when you take turns being "it." As an alternative to running around yourself, try this: Get a flashlight, aim its beam on the floor, and have your child jump on it. Keep moving the beam, and watch your child skip and jump after it.

developing small muscle coordination

earning to use his fingers in a controlled way is major development of the toddler years. These activities focus your child's attention on using the small muscles of his hands:

1 **drawing** Provide a variety of media, from chunky chalk to slim crayons.

2 **block building** Building upwards requires eye-hand coordination as well as precision.

3 **modeling with clay** Toddlers particularly enjoy the squishy feeling that clay provides.

4 **cooking** Joining you in the kitchen has multiple learning benefits.

5 **sewing** Sewing cards especially designed for toddlers offer a fun way to practice focusing on details.

6 **sand building** Using tools or just his hands provides a terrific sensory experience.

7 **playing music** A toy piano, drum, or other musical instrument hones your child's sense of rhythm as well as his coordination.

backyard and playground safety tips

o develop their bodies and their minds, children need wide-open spaces in which they and their imaginations can run wild. To make sure that your outdoor play area is safe:

1 **choose age-appropriate playground equipment** Whether in your backyard gym or at the playground, direct your child to well-made equipment that is suit-

able for her age. Also check that all equipment is designed with safety in mind. For instance, steps on slide ladders must be spaced so that they do not present an entrapment hazard (a space of less than three inches or greater than eight inches).

2 check play equipment for safe positioning
Swings must be away from walls, trees, and high-traffic areas and two feet apart from one another to prevent collisions; slides must empty into low-traffic areas.

3 check all equipment before use
Metal surfaces of slides and swings and other equipment can become burning hot in the summer. In the cold, your child's skin could stick to a metal surface. Touch equipment to be sure it's not too hot or cold before letting your child use it. Check that all equipment is sturdy and free from splinters, loose bolts, and jagged edges.

4 ensure a soft landing
The ground under playground equipment, including backyard gyms, should consist of sand or loose mulch about 12 inches deep, or be covered in foamlike tiles or rubber mats.

5 teach your child to use equipment correctly
Playground equipment is made to be used in a certain way and can be dangerous if not used appropriately. For example, a swing can turn upside down if your child swings on it while standing up.

6 dress your child appropriately
for outdoor play Avoid hoods or scarves that can get tangled in equipment. Long pants and sleeves help protect knees and elbows as well as provide sun protection. Hats offer warmth in winter and shade in summer.

7 the area should be fenced in
A secure gate should surround toddler play areas. No climbable objects such as chairs should line the perimeter of the fence.

8 supervise
Nothing takes the place of adult supervision.

sandbox safety

a sandbox can offer hours of fun for young children. Unfortunately, most public playgrounds do not offer the level of sanitation that is optimal. If your child plays in a public sandbox, be sure to wash her hands and toys thoroughly afterward. Also work with local community groups to monitor the quality of the sand. To help safeguard your child from sandbox hazards in your own backyard:

1 check the quality of the sand Change the sand in your backyard sandbox yearly using light tan, sterilized sand. (Don't buy white, powdery, artificial sand made of crushed rock. It may contain asbestos.)

2 keep your sandbox in a sunny spot Sunlight kills microorganisms. At playtime, position an umbrella to protect your child from the rays.

3 cover the sandbox at night If you live in an area in which animals wander at night, it's a good idea to place a screen or other cover over the box. Don't let your family cat play in the sandbox, since he will likely leave a deposit.

4 avoid lead paint If you have an older home that may have been painted with lead paint, position the sandbox at least ten feet from the base of the house.

5 use a sifter Check regularly for unwanted contents.

teaching math and science

toddler math games

from around the age of two, your child is developmentally ready to understand the one-to-one relationship between a numeral and objects, knowing, for instance, that two is more than one. To help prepare your child for a true understanding of math:

1 count together Counting fingers and toes from one to ten is particularly fun when accompanied by rhymes such as "one, two, buckle my shoe."

2 sort objects Helping your child put things in like categories aids in his understanding of groups. For instance, have him separate his toy cars from his toy airplanes and then count how many are in each group.

3 set the table Setting one plate (preferably non-breakable) for one person, two cups for two people, and so on helps your toddler learn important math skills.

4 name shapes The naming of shapes is fundamental to your child's understanding of math. Play a game of finding squares and circles in your house or on outings. Show how triangles can fit together to make a square.

5 teach spatial relationships Play games that require your child to understand the concepts of near and far or under and over. Let him practice learning such concepts as volume and quantity by filling cups and bowls with water or sand and transferring contents from one container to another.

6 compare sizes Ask your child to find his big bear and his little doll. Line up his trucks from smallest to largest. Play a game in which your child stretches to be as big as he can be and then curls up to make himself tiny.

7 teach patterns Let your child arrange blocks in alternating color or shape patterns.

8 use math concept words Phrases that denote quantity, like "a lot" and "a few," begin to take on meaning when used in everyday conversations.

science for kids

Children are natural scientists, observing their world, testing their hypotheses, and studying the results of their experiments. To help engage your child's natural curiosity:

1 prepare foods together The kitchen makes a great laboratory where your child can observe how mixing ingredients creates new colors and flavors and how heat and cold change the properties of food.

2 plant a garden While it's not a good idea to engage your child in outdoor gardening while you're working with chemicals or seeds that could be accidentally ingested, small-scale and indoor gardening can enthrall your child. Try planting something with a fast growing time, such as an avocado seed or a sweet potato in a clear glass of water, supported with toothpicks inserted in the sides. Within days, your child can witness the growth of roots and soon a few leaves, too.

3 work with water Pouring water is, in itself, a fun activity for your toddler. Also let your child see what happens when you add things to water. What happens if you add a drop of food coloring to water? When you put it in the freezer? What happens to a shallow dish of water if you leave it outside on a warm night? Did a bird drink it? Did it disappear into the air? Let her see that some things, such as salt, dissolve, while others, such as cooking oil, do not.

4 get a close-up look and feel Encourage your child to examine a flower close up, to use a magnifying glass to study an object, and to use her hands to explore textures, such as the bark of a tree.

5 experiment with sound Help your child practice making soft and loud sounds. Show her how talking into an object such as a paper cup changes the sound. Let her put a paper cup to her ear to experience the muffled sounds that result.

6 try tactile games Place a few common objects with different shapes and textures such as a spoon, a mitten, and an ice cube into a bag and ask your child to reach in and try to guess what she's holding without looking.

7 study insects and animals Take a walk in a garden and point out such things as ants and caterpillars. Let your child visually examine them and, with safe species, let your child gently handle them. At a trip to the zoo, talk about animals that fly, walk, or swim. How are baby animals like or different from their parents? Go to a petting zoo where your child can get up close and personal, feeding and touching a variety of critters.

8 watch the sky Point out the wind moving the clouds. Find the moon and stars at night. What colors appear on a clear day, on a cloudy day, at sunset?

9 answer questions with simple answers Don't overwhelm your very young child by going into lengthy, scientific explanations when answering her questions. For instance, if she asks why the sky is blue, simply answer, "Nature made it blue because it's such a pretty color," or "Everything has a color and the sky's color is blue."

teaching your child about color

earning the color properties of objects and ways to create color is sure to fascinate your toddler. To add some color to his experiences:

1 encourage coloring and painting Exposure to a rainbow of colors whets your child's interest in learning color names and other aspects of color, such as shading.

2 celebrate colors Make learning about colors even more fun by having "color days," on which your child wears clothes of a certain color. Then go on a color hunt to find examples of that color throughout the day.

3 mix colors Using finger-paints or water paints, let your child experiment with mixing colors, making green by mixing yellow and blue; making orange by mixing red and yellow, and so on.

4 play stop and go Teach that some colors such as red and green have meanings in stop signs and traffic signals. Play a game: Hold up a green square of construction paper to signal your child to run and a red square to signal him to stop.

5 sort by color When doing the laundry or putting away toys together, group items according to color, including such color concepts as "light" and "dark."

the media

great videos to enjoy with your child

a toddler's love for repetition is fulfilled when she gets to watch her favorite video again and again. Many feature familiar characters. Some give children an up-close look at things that interest them. And others are fun for family viewing. In addition to videos based on your child's favorite TV and book characters, some of the very best are:

series:

1 **Horton Hears a Who!** (Dr. Seuss Series)

2 **Are You My Neighbor?** (Veggie Tales Series)

3 **Very Silly Songs** (Veggie Tales Series)

4 **Wee Sing in Sillyville** (Wee Sing Series)

5 **Cinderella** (Faerie Tale Theatre)

6 **Winnie the Pooh: Seasons of Giving** (Walt Disney Series)

special interest:

7 **Road Construction Ahead**

8 **There Goes a Fire Truck**

9 **Baby Animals** (Natural Heritage)

10 **Really Wild Animals** (National Geographic)

general interest:

11 **The Brave Little Toaster**

12 **The Snowman**

13 **Kristen's Fairy House**

14 **Little Bear: Meet Little Bear**

family viewing:

tv or not tv

There's no doubt that some well-done TV programs and videos can offer education and relaxation. To make the most of your viewing time:

1 choose programs together Each week, review the television guide and pick out programs that look suitable and appealing to your child. Post a chart to remind you of the dates and times near the TV.

2 snuggle up TV watching can become a very lonely and hypnotic event, so even if you're not inclined to get caught up in the action, sit beside your child while you catch up on your own reading or even your bill paying. This way, you can keep alert to the contents so you'll know which programs seem worthwhile for next week's planning.

3 talk about the characters and events Where did Blue hide her bone? Where are Bert and Ernie going on the plane? Young children love to share their understanding of what they're viewing, and talking about a show boosts their egos as well as their vocabularies.

4 draw favorite characters Encourage your child to grab a purple (or other color) crayon to create her own Barney portrait. Be careful not to insist that her drawing look like the professionally rendered illustrations.

5 write to a character Let your child dictate a letter for you to send to a favorite TV character, perhaps simply a fan letter or a question about the character or the technology of the show. You can reach the characters of most shows through the station that carries the program or the production company.

6 act out events If a particular scene elicits a strong response from your child, jot down the dialogue for later acting out. Put together simple costumes and invite some friends over as an audience. Or make finger puppets of the characters by using cutout pictures attached to paper rings.

7 write a book Cut out pictures of TV characters from magazines and television guides and help your child create her own TV guidebook, complete with dictated reviews of favorite programs.

8 play games Cover the screen with a towel and guess which character is talking. Or, while watching the picture, press the mute button and try to guess what the characters are saying.

limit tv and video viewing

because too much TV and video viewing can lead to passivity and obesity, it's best to limit your child's exposure to no more than two hours a day. Here's how:

1 place the TV in an out-of-the-way place Or at least behind the closed doors of a console. When the TV dominates the living area, it tends to dominate family time, too.

2 watch specific programs Know in advance what program you're tuning in to instead of just channel surfing. When that program is over, turn off the set.

3 don't let your child watch adult-oriented TV The contents of news programs, talk shows, and action adventures can frighten your toddler, especially when viewed before bedtime. Save your own viewing until your child is in bed.

4 **have alternatives on hand** TV should not be the first remedy for boredom. Make sure your child has plenty of engaging toys and the company of others to occupy his time.

great computer games for your baby or toddler

earning to navigate a computer game can be loads of fun, provided you choose programs wisely, avoiding drill-and-practice types of programs. These are designed with curious tots in mind:

1 **Reader Rabbit Playtime for Baby** The Learning Company (Ages 9 months to 2 years) Win/Mac.

2 **Reader Rabbit Playtime for Toddler** The Learning Company (Ages 2 to 4 years) Win/Mac.

3 **Sesame Street: Toddler** The Learning Company (Ages 2 to 4 years) Win/Mac.

4 **Teletubbies 2: Favorite Games** Havas Interactive (Ages 12 months to 4 years) Windows.

5 **Dr. Seuss Toddler** Creative Wonders (Ages 18 months to 3 years) Win/Mac.

6 **Winnie the Pooh Toddler** Disney Interactive (Ages 18 months to 3 years) Win/Mac.

7 **Jump Start Baby** Knowledge Adventures (Ages 9 months to 2 years) Win/Mac.

8 **Jump Start Toddlers** Knowledge Adventures (Ages 2 to 4 years) Win/Mac.

notes on music

exposure to music, in addition to being just plain fun, helps develop your child's coordination, sense of rhythm, and math abilities. When sharing music with your child:

1 introduce variety Mix Mozart with reggae, rock with jazz. Expose your child to a rich variety of musical styles, including music written and performed just for kids.

2 have instruments available The freedom to touch and play with both real and toy instruments teaches your child a multitude of lessons, from the science of sound to offering practice in small-motor coordination.

3 watch the volume Blasting music can seriously and permanently harm your child's hearing. Don't allow your child to listen to music with earphones, unless you can be certain she won't turn up the volume to a dangerous level.

4 expose your child to live music Attend child-friendly concerts together so your child can see and hear a performance in action. For your child's sake and the sake of the rest of the audience, however, don't have your child attend a performance intended for a more mature audience.

5 hold off on lessons Most kids aren't ready for formal lessons until at least age five. While some programs designed just for toddlers can be beneficial, don't insist that your child participate unless the interest in learning an instrument is truly hers.

early education

your child's learning styles

Young children learn primarily by using all their senses to discover things about the objects around them as they play. Most tend to favor one or more distinct learning styles, though each child is likely to use all at one time or another. Educators have identified the following seven ways of learning:

1 linguistic This child is keyed in to words, understanding syntax and subtleties in the language more readily than his peers. He enjoys hearing stories and can retell a story as well as create his own. Puns and rhymes hold his interest. He'll learn best by listening and talking, and when he's older, by reading.

2 logical/mathematical This learner has skill with numbers and recognizes patterns easily, noticing, for instance, that his bed quilt contains alternating yellow triangles and red squares. He enjoys learning facts and can compare information to create new ideas. He's most likely to learn to read through phonics, which presents a logical approach to decoding.

3 musical A musical learner is usually able to sing on key and has a natural sense of rhythm. He may be drawn to music, easily mimicking tunes he's heard, even tapping out songs on a piano without having been formally taught. He will learn best when ideas are presented in a musical way. For instance, he may decode words more easily by reading the words to a familiar song or learn to count by sing-songing the numbers in a rhythmic way.

4 spatial A spatial learner is drawn to blocks, clay, paints, and other materials he can manipulate as his best means of learning. He'll easily identify shapes and will, for instance, recognize that two right triangles can form a square. He'll learn his letters by handling three-dimensional forms, such as refrigerator magnets.

5 interpersonal The interpersonal learner is quick to recognize the moods and feelings of others. He enjoys company and makes friends easily. He learns best through interaction with others.

6 intrapersonal This child is very self-aware and can express his feelings, his likes and dislikes, his fears and frustrations readily. He learns best in an environment that supports his emotions. Later on in school, he'll likely keep a diary in which to reflect upon his ups and downs.

7 kinesthetic Physical activity appeals to this child. He'll use his hands skillfully and may show early athletic promise. He enjoys learning most when he can use his body, like learning to count while he jumps.

preschool safety checks

o ensure that any day-care center, preschool, or nursery school you choose is safe, ask yourself:

1 what's the ratio of adults to children? Are there enough adults to be able to get all of the children out of the building quickly, if necessary?

2 how are emergencies handled? Check for such things as smoke detectors and a well-stocked first-aid cabinet. Make sure that at least one person trained in first aid and CPR is always on hand.

3 is food handled correctly? Do staff members wash their hands before handling food and after assisting children with toileting? Are running water, soap, and paper towels readily available? Are perishable foods stored properly in a refrigerator to which children do not have access?

4 are toilets clean and easily accessible? They should be designed for children to use as independently as possible. The sink thermostat should be set so that water cannot be above 120 degrees F to prevent scalding. Are children taught and helped to wash their hands after using the toilet?

5 are changing areas safe and germ-free? If staff members change diapers, are the changing tables sturdy and safe? Do staffers thoroughly clean surfaces and their hands after every change?

6 are the facilities childproofed? All electrical outlets should be covered with safety plugs. Breakable and potentially dangerous materials, such as art supplies and scissors, should be out of reach when not in use. Are there gates on stairways and guards on windows? Are all cleaning products stored in their original containers in locked cabinets?

7 is play equipment clean and in good condition?

what a nursery school should teach

nursery or preschool is usually where two- and three-year olds have their first formal learning experiences. In a good early-education program, your child will learn to:

1 form attachments with others outside his family Regularly seeing the same adults and children places your child in a community in which he will learn to develop appropriate relationships.

2 hone social skills Both teacher prompts and peer behavior will help your child learn to share, take turns, and respect another's space and point of view.

3 practice physical activities Most families don't have the space and equipment to allow toddlers the freedom of movement that a good preschool program does.

4 practice creative arts Similarly, few families have a comparable range of art and music supplies for their children to work with.

5 increase language skills While family members may be adept at understanding a toddler, those in his new circle may require that he polish his pronunciation and increase his vocabulary to be understood.

6 an introduction to pre-academic skills A good program does not focus on letters or numbers for their own sake, but introduces concepts that will foster later learning, such as learning colors and shapes, and listening attentively to a story.

7 increased independence and self-care skills

Putting on his own coat, storing his supplies in his own cubby, and other gestures of responsibility help your child learn independence.

8 cultural literacy
Learning the songs and games that others are likely to know helps prepare your child for further learning and socialization.

evaluating a nursery school

In addition to factors such as convenience and cost, when you're looking for an appropriate program for your child:

1 check out supplies and equipment
Are there a variety of art materials and toys, and is playground equipment in good working order? Be cautious if you see toys with broken or missing pieces, few crayons, limited art materials, and books with torn pages or missing covers, for example. Look for different sizes and kinds of paper, whether the crayons and paint-brushes are the right size for small hands, and good supplies of paint and clay. Check that there is space and appropriate material for creative activities in art, music, blocks, sand, and water play.

2 ask the director about her own goals
and educational ideas Talk about what she likes best about the job. Ask how she communicates her goals to the classroom teachers, and discuss their experience. Adults trained in child development or early-childhood education make better preschool teachers.

3 ask the director about other parents
Listen to whether the director describes them positively or negatively. Don't hesitate to ask for references.

4 talk with the teacher about the program
Ask about the type of activities and the skills taught. Determine how play figures into the program. Free play should be balanced with organized play activities.

5 note the ratio of children to teachers
There should be one adult for every four to six two-year-

olds and one adult for every seven to eight three-year-olds. Check that the adults on staff actually spend time with the children and not in administrative positions; find out what the school's policy is when a teacher is absent: Is a substitute provided?

6 observe a class in action Look at the children and the teachers. Note whether children appear busy and happy or overwhelmed or bored. Notice if each child is engaged and if everyone is doing the same thing, or if small groups are doing different activities.

7 look at the setup of the classroom Try to see the facilities and play areas through your child's eyes. There should be lots of ongoing projects that might include making simple recipes, working with puppets, and planting and tending bean seeds. If children are expected to sit at desks and do teacher-directed activities in workbooks, there won't be much time for creative exploration. Are there comfortable spaces for different ways of learning? For example, can the children sit on the floor for storytime? Is there room on the walls for children's artwork? Remember, a place that is too tidy may actually be too controlled to accommodate children's activities.

8 interview the teacher Ask about her discipline policy. Note her attitude when she talks about children. While observing the class, watch while the teacher actually disciplines a child, if possible. Her interactions should be positive and accepting of both the victim and the transgressor.

9 observe how the teacher interacts How does she relate to your child when you visit? She should be respectful of your child's temperament, helping a clingy, boisterous, shy, or wound-up child feel welcome.

10 how are new students greeted? What kind of transition time is allowed? Can you stay with your child during the first few days?

11 ask how toileting accidents are handled A child should never be made to feel ashamed of such an event.

12 above all, ask yourself: Would *I* would want to spend time here?

easing your child's separation anxiety

Starting a nursery or preschool program necessarily means spending time away from you. Some kids skip happily off to this new adventure. Many others require special handling to ease their concerns about being separated. To help your child take this big step:

1 develop a ritual for leave-taking For example, each morning before your leave your child at school, sing a special song together or develop a private wave or handshake. Such rituals give your child a feeling of control over the situation.

2 talk about something other than departure Focus the conversation on fun things your child will do at school, the weather, her new shoes. Don't reassure her that she'll be fine; too much reassurance makes her think there really is cause for worry.

3 offer support, not sympathy If it upsets your child when you leave, don't get too emotional yourself. Be positive and supportive, but remind her that her job is to go to school. Don't get angry; do be firm.

4 bring something special from home If the school allows children to bring toys or other things from home, be sure that your child has a comforting object to tote along with her.

5 always allow enough time A rushed departure can unnerve even a child who has not had particular difficulty letting go.

travel and everyday outings

car and public transportation travel

choosing and using a car seat

C ar seats are essential for any travel with children and are required by law for infants and toddlers, yet a recent study shows that 85 percent of safety seats are used incorrectly. Before buying and installing your car seat:

1 decide on an infant, toddler, or convertible seat You can purchase a seat designed especially for an infant under 20 pounds and 26 inches in height, one designed solely for toddlers above 20 pounds and over 26 inches, or a seat that converts from infant to toddler use. If you choose a convertible seat, invest in a padded insert to keep your newborn secure and comfortable. If your child is over 40 pounds, he's ready for a booster seat.

2 be sure your infant seat reclines all the way This is the safest position for newborns.

3 use a new seat, if possible Safety standards are always being improved, so a new seat is usually your best investment. If you are using a hand-me-down, call the manufacturer to make sure that the model has not been recalled and request a copy of the installation instructions if you don't already have them. Never use a seat that has been in an accident since it may have unseen structural defects.

4 follow the manufacturer's guidelines Also follow any special instructions from your car's manufacturer. Common installation errors include too-loose shoulder and waist straps on the car seat; vehicle seat belts that are improperly threaded through the car seat underside; and seat belts that are too slack to hold the car seat securely. The seat should be wedged in firmly against your vehicle's seat. When properly installed, it won't move more than an inch in any direction at the base.

5 keep instructions handy Place the installation instructions in an envelope and tape it to the underside of the car seat so that you'll have them available if you move the seat from one vehicle to another.

6 install the seat well before needing it The hospital parking lot is not the place to figure out how to install the seat safely. Do it a few weeks before your due date.

7 face infants toward the back Face older babies and toddlers forward. Babies under six months of age or 20 pounds and 26 inches in length should be seated facing the rear because it is safest. Older babies and toddlers over 20 pounds or 26 inches are uncomfortable sitting backwards—their legs don't fit—so they should be seated facing forward.

8 put the car seat in the middle of the back seat In a van with three rows of seats, the best place is the middle of the middle row.

9 check points of contact An infant seat should have three points of contact: two shoulder straps and a crotch strap or an overhead shield with a locking buckle. A convertible seat should have five points of contact: two shoulder straps, two for the waist, and one for the crotch.

10 stay informed If you have any questions about the proper installation of your car seat, call SafetyBeltSafe USA at 800-745-7233 or the federal auto-safety hotline at 800-424-9393. The Safe Kids Buckle Up Child Safety Program also offers car seat checkups nationwide. To locate a local checkpoint, call 202-662-0600 or visit their Website at www.safekids.org.

keep your child safe
in the car

n addition to using a car seat correctly, the following can
keep your child safe and comfortable during car trips:

1 drive safely and defensively Aggressive driving,
tailgating, speeding, and ignoring road signs and adverse
conditions create accidents. Never drive while using a
cell phone.

2 use seat belts and never overcrowd a car
Every passenger, not just the children, needs his or her
own seat belt. Never accept more passengers than your
vehicle was designed to carry.

3 watch out for doors Always look to make sure
feet, hands, and belongings are safely inside before
closing doors.

4 watch out for sun and heat Install a sun protector
on the side windows. Before placing your child in her
car seat on a warm day or if the car has been parked in
the sun, check to make sure that the seat and the buckle
are not too hot.

5 insist on good car behavior Never allow rough-
housing, tossing toys, or other distracting behavior
while you're driving. If children misbehave, pull over
and wait until they compose themselves.

6 turn off the engine and lock the doors Always
secure your car when you're not inside it. Toddlers have
been known to slip into the family car and put it in gear.

**7 don't put heavy or sharp objects in the glove
box** A sudden stop could send things hurtling. Use the
trunk, or for vans, secure heavy objects to the frame.

8 never leave your child unattended in a car
Do not get out even to run into a corner store to get a
soda unless you take your children with you.

9 don't eat or play with sharp objects An item like a pencil is dangerous to your child during car trips. She could choke or be injured in case of a sudden stop.

10 never ride in an open truck flatbed This is never safe for your child, even for a short ride.

public transportation

f you live in or visit suburban or urban areas with your child in tow:

1 opt for buses and trains over cabs If you aren't traveling with a portable safety seat, it's best to avoid taxis. Never strap your child into the same seat belt with you.

2 use a front carrier with babies Even if you're using a stroller for part of your trip, it's handy to have your infant in a front carrier if you'll be getting on and off buses. This way your hands will be free.

3 seat your baby on your lap The safest position on a bus or train for a baby is on your lap, facing you.

4 teach public transportation safety and manners Insist that your toddler sit properly in his seat. Have him sit in your lap when the bus or train is crowded, so that others can use the seat. Don't allow your child to run in aisles or to stick his hands or head out the windows.

everyday outings

preparing for baby's first outing

depending on the weather, taking a healthy infant outdoors is fine as early as the first week. When you take your baby on her first tour of the world:

1 avoid crowds Until your baby's immune system is better able to fight off infection, usually at about six weeks, stay away from crowds.

2 dress your baby comfortably With the exception of adding a lightweight knit hat on warm days, or an additional layer on cold days, dress your baby as you dress yourself for the weather. Layers are always a good idea since you can add or subtract clothing as the temperature changes.

3 provide sun protection Be sure your baby's delicate skin is protected from the sun's rays. (See page 73 for information about avoiding sunburn.)

4 keep out the wind and cold Invest in a wind and rain cover for your baby's stroller or pram. If she must go outside on a very cold day, protect her face by loosely draping a scarf or a light blanket around her face, being sure not to restrict her breathing. A thin layer of petroleum jelly on her cheeks will help prevent chapping. Do not let wind blow directly on your child's face since it can interfere with breathing.

5 make early outings short Don't overwhelm yourself or your baby with long hours out. Keep outings short until you're comfortable with your baby, how to work her stroller, and how much gear to cart along.

diaper bag essentials

keep your diaper bag clean, stocked, and, except for perishable foods, ready to go. Choose a bag that has separate compartments for food and clothing, and that has a changing pad—one that's waterproof and has a wide, comfortable strap. (Diaper backpacks are great because they free your arms.) Stock it with:

1 **several diapers** Trust that one will never be enough.

2 **wipes** Use a portable container or plastic bag.

3 **a well-insulated bottle** Bring two if your child is bottle-fed.

4 **a change of clothing**

5 **a lightweight blanket**

6 **a bib**

7 **snacks and drinks** For an older toddler.

8 **toys and books**

9 **a business card or other identification**

public-place safety

While you can't childproof the entire world, taking these precautions while on outings with your child can keep you both safe:

1 **always scan your area for hazards** Be alert to open chutes, swinging or automatic doors, slippery floors, and uneven or broken pavement.

2 **identify exits immediately** Whenever you're in an enclosed space, such as a mall, restaurant, or theater, know where the emergency exits are located.

3 **avoid deserted and overcrowded places**

4 **teach your kid to stay put if you get separated** Ideally, your child should be safely in a stroller or

holding your hand in a public place. However, in a playground, he probably has freer rein. If the two of you should happen to get separated, teach him to remain in one place and to wait for you to find him.

5 carry a portable phone If you've got a cell phone, keep it charged and with you on outings.

what you should know about carriers

front carriers or backpack-style carriers can be a real comfort and convenience. Keep in mind:

1 front packs are best for newborns In addition to freeing your hands, front carriers offer your baby security and comfort.

2 don't use back carriers at first Wait until your baby is at least six months old and can hold up his head.

3 try out different styles before purchasing
Parents tend to have strong preferences for front or sling-style infant carriers. If possible, borrow various carriers and try them out before you purchase. Keep in mind that you and your partner may prefer different models—and that for some models, you can purchase a second set of larger or smaller straps.

4 don't overuse carriers They can strain your back.

choosing a stroller or pram

prams, in which a baby lies down, are best for babies under six months of age. Once your baby can sit up on her own, switch to a stroller. Don't use a stroller with a soft back for infants, and don't let a child who can sit up use a pram, since she could easily fall out. Some models convert from pram to stroller. Here's what to look for:

1 choose a stroller or pram with a wide base
You want to be sure that the carrier cannot tip over.

2 only use a stroller with proper restraints
Good restraints should secure your baby at the waist
with a guard between her legs so she can't slide out.

3 check the brakes They should be secure and easy
to operate.

4 be sure it has the storage capacity you need
Opt for a stroller or pram with a basket under the seat,
which will offer more stability than a basket at the rear.

5 test the height of the handles The handles
should be at a comfortable height.

6 check the wheels Rubber wheels are generally
easier to maneuver than plastic. Bigger wheels roll over
rough terrain more easily. Try out the wheels on a
variety of surfaces to be sure of a smooth ride.

7 examine the overall construction Are bolts in
tightly? If foldable, is it easy to operate? Open and close
it a few times to ensure that latches are secure. Are all
parts free from sharp edges?

8 opt for a washable fabric

using a stroller or pram

a lways follow these safety tips when transporting your
child in a stroller or pram:

1 always use the restraining system

2 never allow a child to stand

3 never leave your baby unattended

4 don't sling heavy parcels over the handle This
could tip the stroller.

5 watch out for your child's fingers Keep all body
parts clear when folding a collapsible stroller.

6 don't allow your older child to ride behind
your baby in a stroller meant for one child. Never sit an
older child in an infant's pram.

preschool pedestrian safety

these rules apply, of course, to just about everyone, but you'll need to be obvious about following them when you're out with your toddler:

1 set a good example Your child will notice if you race across the street against the light. Cross only at the corner or a pedestrian crosswalk and always obey the lights.

2 state what you're doing aloud Explain that you stop, look, and listen before crossing the street.

3 stop at driveways Teach your child to notice driveways as well as corners and to follow the "stop, look, and listen" rule.

4 hold hands when crossing the street Insist on this practice every time.

5 don't allow play in the street or driveway Even if you live in a quiet cul-de-sac, don't let your child play in a place in which cars travel.

6 teach your child about cars Explain to him that even though he can see a car, the driver may not be able to see him.

7 don't run Teach your child to walk, not run, across the street.

8 be attentive to emergency vehicles Ambulances and other emergency vehicles may not stop fully at red lights or might not follow traffic rules. Look both ways when crossing one-way streets, since a car may be backing up or traveling the wrong way.

9 wear bright, reflective clothing At night and on gray days, being highly visible is especially important.

10 walk on the left Face the traffic when walking on country roads.

11 avoid puddles if you can't see the bottom Avoid storm drains.

shopping trips

avoiding falls and entrapment

1 always carry your baby or young toddler

2 check for tied shoelaces Also be sure your child's pants and coats don't drag.

3 teach your older toddler to face forward Teach her to stand in the center of the step, keeping her feet away from the edges.

4 have your child hold the handrail If she can't reach the handrail, she should hold your hand.

5 going down, stand in front of your toddler Show her how to get off at the bottom.

6 going up, stand behind your child Guide her off a the top.

7 never take a stroller onto an escalator Use the elevator if you have a stroller or shopping cart.

8 use the shutoff button in case of emergency An emergency shutoff is usually located at both the top and bottom of the escalator, near the handrail.

local outings

When you've had your fill of playgrounds and at-home playdates, consider these excursions and activities:

1 go wild Even if there's no zoo in your immediate area, check out other venues for viewing wildlife—and domesticated animals, too, such as a neighborhood pet store. Call ahead and see if a local vet will allow you and your child to visit.

2 watch products being made What stores in the neighborhood create their products in-house? Your toddler can enjoy watching pizza or bread in the making, shoes being repaired, or the latest work at a construction sight.

3 meet neighborhood helpers Visit the local firehouse, where your toddler may even get a chance to try on a firefighter's helmet or sit in the big truck.

4 explore Think about the places right in your neighborhood that you've never been inside or that are not generally appropriate places to visit with your toddler. For instance, if your child is not yet ready to view a film in a movie house, he might still enjoy looking around between shows. Ask the attendant if you can take a free five-minute tour. Or visit houses of worship that are not your own, when services are not going on. Your child will enjoy the new sights and scents.

5 reverse the seasons Visit a beach in the winter or a ski resort in summer, if either happens to be nearby.

6 adopt a tree or a particular nest or a patch of garden. Visit every day to see what's new and to talk about any changes.

7 make a path Take a walk and leave behind a trail of bread, stones, or other organic material. Then follow your path back.

8 record your day Take instant photos and make a book about your day. Let your child pose at various stops and then dictate information about it for you to write down. Paste the pictures and words in a notebook or on construction paper and read the story back later in the day. Or videotape a tour of the neighborhood to play back.

9 have a picnic You don't have to wait for a long weekend with lots of people around to enjoy dining out. Pack a blanket and some easy-to-serve treats and head to the local park.

10 be silly Take a backward walk while wearing backward shirts. Or let your child dress in a costume, such as a lion, and use the neighborhood backdrop as your jungle.

shopping cart safety

t he top-heavy design of most shopping carts makes them inherently dangerous. To minimize the hazards:

1 use a built-in infant seat when available Be sure to strap your child in securely and double-check that the seat is firmly attached to the cart. If an infant seat is not available in the cart, do not place your child in the basket seat until his sitting-up skills are well developed. Instead, use a front carrier to hold your baby while you shop. Never attach a car or infant seat to the cart.

2 always use the restraining belt If the stores in which you shop don't have carts with built-in straps, purchase a harness strap in a juvenile products store and carry it with you whenever you take your child shopping.

3 never allow your child to sit or stand in the main body of the cart.

4 don't allow your toddler to ride along the outside of the cart, or to push the cart.

5 never leave your child unattended in a shopping cart.

standing in line

Waiting can be rough when you're a toddler, especially in the checkout aisle at the grocery store. Here are ways to distract your child and have some fun:

1 find colors Take turns finding red things, then green things, and so on.

2 read a book Keep short books on hand for just this purpose.

3 identify foods Ask your child to point to foods you name in your cart or to name foods for you to point to.

4 play Simon says In the toddler version, no one loses. Simply help your child enjoy following directions such as "Simon says, 'Put your hand on your head.'"

5 sing a song It beats listening to Musak and gives your child practice in recalling lyrics of familiar tunes.

vacations away from home

the friendly skies

taking an infant or toddler on a plane ride can be exciting—or exasperating. It all depends on your sense of humor and how well you've prepared. Here are five tips to get you on your way:

1 plan ahead When booking your flight, try to arrange for bulkhead seats (the first row behind first class). These provide more leg room and are easier to get into and out of. Book a window seat if your child is likely to be enthralled by the view, but an aisle seat if she's more inclined to need bathroom breaks. Aim for flying at times of the day when your child is likely to be sleeping soundly or wide awake and in a good mood. Also, if possible, fly at less popular times to insure more patient assistance. And dress your child comfortably. If you want her to be wearing something cute when she greets Grandma at the arrival gate, change her at the end of the flight.

2 properly restrain your child For safety's sake, even if your child is young enough to ride free in your lap, book her her own seat and keep her in it for the duration of the flight, which could save her life in case of turbulence. Check with the airline to be sure that your child's car seat meets with federal air-travel regulations. If it doesn't, see if the airline can provide an acceptable child-safety seat. Keep your child buckled in throughout the flight, except for necessary bathroom breaks.

3 avoid earaches If your child has even the slightest head congestion, takeoffs and landings can cause pressure to build up in the ear canal, which results in painful earaches. The best remedy is to have her sucking during ascents and descents. If your infant is breast-feeding exclusively, practice using a bottle a few days before the trip so that you can feed her without removing her from her safety eat. Toddlers can drink from a juice box or suck on a lollipop. If your child has an ear infection or symptoms of a cold, check with your pediatrician before flying.

4 make meals fun If your child is old enough to eat the snacks or meal that the airline provides, call a day before the flight to request the special child's fare. Many airlines provide fun boxed meals and your child will feel special receiving this extra service. Since many domestic flights no longer serve meals on board, be sure to have something nutritious packed, even if you think your child can wait until landing to eat. Delays can put many hours between lunch and dinner, and a hungry child is a very unhappy traveler. Also, during the flight, make sure your child drinks lots of noncarbonated, no-caffeine drinks to keep from getting dehydrated.

5 pay attention to carry-ons In addition to snacks, include in your carry-on a change of clothes for your child, all medications anyone in your family may need (you can't always get to your checked luggage when you need to), and quiet distractions for your child – coloring books and crayons, a tape player with some songs and story tapes, books, and a plush toy or favorite blanky to cuddle with during naps.

amusing your backseat passenger

ong car trips can exasperate young travelers. Try these ideas to keep your child comfortable and occupied:

1 have toys available Use plastic chains (never strings or ropes that could strangle your child) to attach toys to the car seat so that your child can retrieve any dropped item on his own.

2 play audio story tapes or kid-friendly music Or, if your car or van has a video player, insert a tape.

3 play simple games Along with your child, count how many blue cars, flagpoles, or school buses you see along the way.

4 stop frequently Every two hours or so, stop at a playground or park and let your child run around to unleash some pent-up energy. Take frequent breaks for infants, too, for feeding, changing, and relaxing.

5 provide a neck rest Invest in a baby- or toddler-size neck rest so your child can nap comfortably.

6 keep your child hydrated Though it will mean more bathroom stops for just-trained toddlers, it's important that your child drink lots of noncarbonated, unsweetened liquids to prevent dehydration. Water is best. Consider purchasing a portable potty for use on your travels.

7 offer familiar foods A road trip is not the best place to introduce your child to the local cuisine. Pack some favorite foods to enjoy along the way.

8 dress your child comfortably Pack a few clean tee shirts and change into fresh ones every so often, which will make your child feel far more comfortable. Make the last change of the evening into pajamas so that when you arrive at your destination, your child can get to bed with less fuss.

9 go barefoot If it's not cold in the car, let your child take off his shoes and socks while inside.

10 have a toy treat bag Invest in some car-safe toys such as crayons and coloring books to dole out in the course of your journey.

11 start a collection To help get your older toddler in the mood to look forward to each stop and start, create a collection of free or inexpensive souvenirs. For instance, collect paper placemats from each restaurant you visit or buy a postcard at each stop.

precautions for small guests

Visiting friends and relatives is a great way to socialize your child. To help make your visits safe:

1 conduct a quick childproofing review Are stairs blocked? Are medicines, cleaning products, and break-ables out of reach? Are electrical cords safely put away? Are sockets filled with safety plugs? Are windows closed at the bottom? Is access to decks and balconies restricted?

Look around and correct or at least be on heightened alert for potential dangers.

2 have familiar and new toys available Having playthings with which your child is comfortable as well as something new to hold her interest can help prevent your child from undue exploring to entertain herself.

3 cart along a safe space If you'll be spending any time in another's home, consider packing a playpen, even if you generally don't use one, so that you have a safe space for your child.

planning a family vacation

aking off with a toddler in tow offers particular pleasures and challenges. Keep in mind:

1 the vacation is for everyone Plan on some activities with each family member, including your baby or toddler. Far more enjoyable for your child is a few hours of your unhurried time than a tour of local landmarks.

2 don't try to do too much You'll find yourself and your child much more relaxed if you don't plan more than one or two distinct activities per day. Rushing from place to place to see or do too much will simply leave everyone frazzled.

3 take short breaks from one another Many resorts offer high-quality child care options, in which you can entrust your child to staff who can offer age-appropriate fun while you do something that's best enjoyed without your child.

4 don't forget important papers In addition to travel documents such as passports and tickets, be sure to carry along copies of prescriptions for medications, phone numbers of your pediatrician and other doctors, and numbers of all hotels or motels into which you've booked a room so that you can confirm your arrival. The last thing you need is to show up and find that you're without a place to stay.

on the road

One of the pleasures of traveling is the chance to break from routine. For your child, however, familiar patterns continue to offer comfort.

1 stick to bedtime and feeding schedules If full meals aren't possible at regular mealtimes, be sure to offer your child a snack. Don't schedule fun events for usual naptimes.

2 carry the familiar with you A few choice toys, a stuffed animal, and a lovey from home can make the unfamiliar less daunting to your toddler.

3 stick to your established bedtime routine
Even if you can't put your child into her own bed at the normal hour, follow the rest of your routine as much as you can—for instance, by reading her favorite bedtime story.

must-have travel products

these items can help make your away-from-home time safer and more pleasant:

1 a travel first-aid kit Include antiseptic wipes, antibiotic ointments, bandages, child and adult fever reducer, a thermometer, and any prescribed medications.

2 a portable stroller Even if your child rarely uses a stroller, you'll want to have one during travel. Walking even the length of an airport gate can be too much for a travel-weary toddler.

3 car seat comforts A sun shield to block out unpleasant rays and a neck rest to keep your toddler comfy during naps in a car or plane are essential.

hotel hints

While hotels and motels offer fewer potential dangers than most homes, keep these tips in mind:

1 book a ground-floor room Ask for one close to the main desk. You'll find it easier to get yourself, your child, and all her gear to and from the room and you'll avoid the trouble that comes with stairs and elevators.

2 carry along easy-to-install safety devices If you're staying for a while, install safety latches on cabinets, drawers, and the bathroom door. (Duct tape and cords that don't hang more than a few inches can substitute for latches. Doorknob covers that prevent your child from turning the knob can also keep kids out of off-limits rooms.) Cover outlets with safety plugs. Wrap any dangling electrical cords and window treatment cords. Be sure windows are closed and locked at the bottom and that your child cannot enter any terrace or deck area without you.

3 check out the room's safety features Is there a smoke detector in the room with a working battery? (You can carry a battery tester with you.) Read the safety warnings posted in the room so you know what to do in the event of a fire or other emergency. Know where your nearest exits are.

4 bring your child's own bedding If the hotel or motel provides a crib, be sure that it meets safety standards. (See page 50.) Bring along a favorite blanket so your child can enjoy the comforting familiarity of his own things while in a strange place.

vacation venues

thinking about trying something a little different? Here's a starting place:

1 family camp Camp is not just for big kids. To help families enjoy the experience together, often complete with nighttime sing-alongs, dozens of camps open their gates to families during off-peak times when big kids have gone back to school. You'll stay in bunks or tents provided by the camp and chow down with other campers, so there's no need to own or know how to use equipment. Call the American Camping Association or the chamber of commerce or tourist board of an area you'd like to see to find out about family-style camps.

2 working vacations Throughout the country, farms and ranches offer "working" vacations to families who want to know what it's like to milk a cow or bale some hay.

3 historic settings Restored or recreated towns that harken back to earlier times offer a particularly enjoyable respite for hurried families. Even young children can marvel at seeing horse-drawn carriages head down Main Street or take part in corn shucking.

4 cruises Ships have become far more family friendly than they once were and many offer the perfect compromise for all family members as well as the convenience of not having to pack and unpack as you go along. Look for a line that offers special deals and activities for young children.

special events

holidays

get a handle on the holidays

the rituals surrounding many holidays make your child feel like part of a larger world and increase his sense of identity. To help make your child's holiday memories happy ones:

1 review your traditions A new baby or a mobile toddler can necessitate some changes in your traditional celebration. Discuss with your family some ideas that take into consideration your energy level and your child's safety.

2 involve your child in satisfying ways But don't push him to cuddle up to relatives he may not feel comfortable with or to pose for pictures in Santa's lap if he'd prefer not to. You'll have plenty of time in the years ahead to integrate your child into the rituals.

3 be aware of extra dangers Holiday candles, scissors used for wrapping gifts, dishes full of candies, alcohol-filled glasses—these and many other items find their way into your child's path at holiday time.

4 don't do it alone Consider hiring help for the holidays, either to watch your child or to take over some tasks that you usually do.

5 respect your child's need for comfort It's tempting to put your daughter into a dress with stiff lace or your son into a cute little suit. This is fine for a few pictures and introductions to rarely seen relatives, but, for the most part, choose soft, comfy clothes over dress-up duds until your child is old enough to enjoy it.

6 maintain schedules as much as possible If you can stick to somewhat normal eating and bedtime routines, your child will be more likely to enjoy the holiday activity.

safe with santa

make sure you're saying, "Ho-Ho," and not "Oh, No!" by following these seasonal safety guidelines:

1 limit your child's access to the tree Place a gate around it. If you have a real tree, regularly vacuum for pine needles.

2 keep kids away from ornaments Hang breakable items near the top of the tree or store them for use when your child is older.

3 follow the instructions for electric lights Use lights designed for outdoors only outside and indoor lights only inside. Check all wires for nicks and crimps, which could cause overheating, and be sure there are lights in every socket to avoid any chance of metal touching the contact point. If wires ever feel hot to the touch, unplug and discard immediately. Never run wires under carpeting, rugs, or radiators, where the insulation could be damaged. Position a smoke detector and a fire extinguisher near the tree.

4 be extra vigilant while entertaining Keep your child in view at all times when candles are burning and food and drink are easily accessible. Store visitors' handbags on a high shelf, where your toddler cannot get into them. Best of all: Plan your home entertaining for after your child is in bed.

5 review packages Check the gifts first before letting your child unwrap on his own. Dispose of ribbons, tape, and any plastic wrapping immediately in an inaccessible trashcan.

6 save certain gifts for later If your child receives gifts that are not age-appropriate, store them until he is older.

limiting halloween nightmares

halloween presents young children with an odd dilemma: It's fun for them to dress up and make believe, but it's sometimes terrifying to watch others do the same. To help your child enjoy Halloween safely:

1 carefully monitor what your child sees While older kids may get a real kick out of walking through a make-believe haunted house or taking a hayride through eerie surroundings, such events are likely to terrify your toddler.

2 introduce masks carefully Most babies and toddlers have an innate fear of masks because reading facial features is one of the ways they understand the world. When features suddenly change, even to benign ones, the whole world can seem scary. If you or older siblings will be wearing masks, introduce the masks carefully, showing it to your child before anyone wears it. Don't insist that she wear a mask.

3 keep your child away from the door Attend to the local trick-or-treating ghouls and goblins by yourself, at least until you've ascertained whether the costumes will frighten her.

4 take part in organized toddler activities Rather than taking your child trick-or-treating with the bigger neighborhood kids, plan an event limited to smaller children and unscary outfits.

5 trick-or-treat in daylight If you do take your child on a neighborhood outing, do so in daylight, when the costumes and decor won't combine with darkness to overwhelm her.

6 talk about real and make-believe Though preschoolers don't often distinguish between what's real and what's not, Halloween offers a good time to introduce the concept of pretending.

7 be alert to dangers Costume your child in well-fitting clothing to avoid tripping and to limit the risk of her costume catching fire near an open flame. Avoid masks, which interfere with vision. Steer clear of candlelit jack-o'-lanterns. Never allow your child to eat any treats she collects until you have thoroughly examined them and removed choking hazards such as gum and hard candies from her haul.

handling holiday company

holidays are a wonderful time to reconnect with family and friends, all of whom, no doubt, feel closer to your child than she does to them.

1 make introductions ahead of time Talk about someone who's coming for a visit. If possible, show your child pictures of the person. Arrange a telephone meeting beforehand.

2 help visitors respect your child's needs Before your great aunt surrounds your toddler with a hug, say something like, "We're so glad to see you, but Lisa needs to get to know you better before she's comfortable getting close. Let's give her a little time."

3 give your child a job Even a toddler can pass out napkins to guests. She will feel important to have been granted such a big responsibility and the gesture will allow her the chance to approach everyone briefly.

4 don't expect too much Your child may be the picture of politeness at family affairs, but a larger crowd may unhinge her. React with understanding and empathy.

5 provide an out Make sure you provide opportunities for your child to have downtime during any gathering so that she doesn't have to try to maintain her dignity longer than necessary.

birthday parties

first-birthday bashes

et's face it: Your newly minted one-year-old doesn't have the faintest idea that it's his birthday. So the party is really for you, and you deserve it. To celebrate:

1 limit the guests Invite adults and one or two other toddlers. Family members and the parents of the kids you've met this year and with whom you've shared so many firsts are good choices.

2 consider kids' schedules Plan the party for when kids are likely to be in a good mood. After naps and feeding times are best so that the guest of honor and his peers are less inclined to fuss.

3 limit the length Plan on one and a half hours from start to finish, so that the party ends before the kids' moods deteriorate.

4 serve kids their usual fare Don't introduce new foods—except, perhaps, a bit of birthday cake—to your toddler guests.

5 get some air Weather permitting, take the birthday baby and younger guests, along with their parents, for a walk midway through the party; let the kids run off steam for 20 minutes or so.

6 video the action Videotape the kids together for a few minutes, getting a few close-ups of their faces. Then play it back for them. Kids this age love seeing the faces of other toddlers, even if they don't recognize the stars of the show as themselves.

parents ALERT!

no latex balloons Broken bits of latex balloons are an extreme choking hazard and should not be used around children under the age of six. Opt for mylar instead. With all balloons, immediately clean up any broken pieces before kids can get their hands on them.

great gifts for ones

One-year-olds are just becoming mobile and their improved eye-hand coordination will allow them to enjoy a wide variety of playthings, including:

1 push and ride-on toys Look for a wide wheelbase to prevent tipping.

2 balls Large, lightweight balls to kick, and plush balls that are designed to be grasped by little fingers meet your child's need for challenges.

3 books Board books and waterproof books for the bath add to your child's home library.

4 stacking toys Toddler-tested stacking toys and soft blocks provide hours of fun and learning.

5 shape sorters and nesting toys These help toddlers learn concentration skills.

6 pretend-play toys Miniature copies of familiar grown-up objects such as toy vacuum cleaners help your toddler enjoy mimicking grown-up behavior.

7 dolls and huggies Cuddly toys bring out your child's nurturing qualities.

8 household objects A plastic tub for water or sand play, measuring spoons, a colander—these household items encourage your child to experiment and discover.

fabulous party favors for one-year-olds

Since your child's guest list will most likely be limited, go all out on favors such as:

1 plastic sand buckets and shovels Fill them with large plastic cookie cutters for sand play.

2 personalized bibs Make them yourself or order them from a photo store.

3 tee shirts If your child is crazy about cars, pick out one with a car design. Or buy or make shirts that announce, "I'm one!"

4 chunky books

5 sippy cups A birthday design will make an extra-special treat.

6 toddler-size fork and spoon sets

terrific ideas for second- and third-birthday parties

ow that your child is a bit more socialized and is likely to have a few friends to call her own, the focus of the party shifts to the guests. In addition to keeping the gathering small (three to six kids and their parents) and keeping the festivities short (no more than two hours, preferably post-nap):

1 serve fun foods Two- and three-year-olds can decorate their own cupcakes with plain icing and sprinkles (other candies might present a choking hazard). Arrange the menu around foods your young guests generally eat; good choices include tea-size sandwiches of jam, tuna, or egg salad. Serve drinks in covered cups with straws. Your best bets for beverages include milk and diluted fruit punch (choose a nonstaining color).

2 play age-appropriate games Set up outdoors, if possible. Opt for games that most of the children are familiar with. At this stage, steer clear of competitive games, adapting old standards so that everyone wins. (For a suggested list of party games, see pages 186–87.)

3 take instant snapshots of the kids arriving Include them in the guests' party-favor bags.

great gifts for two-year-olds

your two-year-old and her peers will enjoying receiving these gifts that encourage continued development of coordination and thinking skills:

1 ride-ons Foot-powered ride-ons are a big hit now. Caution: Never let your toddler ride anywhere near a built-in pool area.

2 musical toys Dancing and making music is a favorite activity for twos.

3 blocks sets Colorful blocks in a variety of shapes encourage two-year-olds to learn about color and shape as they play. Large interlocking blocks such as Duplo are great now.

4 books Picture books with easy-to-turn pages are a hit with this crowd.

5 art materials Paints, brushes, and easels or crayons and loads of paper are perfect now.

6 dress-up clothes Play hats of all kinds and clothes that bear pictures of familiar characters are great fun for kids who are beginning to learn to dress themselves.

7 puppets Let your child act out the stories that are beginning to bloom in his imagination.

8 dolls and stuffed animals These are especially good for comforting your child during transitions, such as bedtime, and to help during separations.

9 grown-up objects for pretend play From toy cash registers to sit-in cars (nonmotorized), kids this age can easily imagine themselves following your lead.

10 tents and play houses Private, covered spaces where your child can act out her imaginative play make your two-year-old feel very special.

great gifts for three-year-olds

Your three-year-old has reached a level of maturity that allows for additions of big-kid toys that challenge her to develop her coordination and thinking skills, such as:

1 ride-ons Now's the time for a small trike with pedals. Caution: Since your three-year-old doesn't yet have the judgment and the consistent coordination to steer and use the brakes properly, careful monitoring is essential. And never let your child ride anywhere near a built-in pool area.

2 puzzles Look for ones with no more than about 12 pieces.

3 large beads and string and/or sewing cards Threes feel proud of their newfound fine motor skills and love opportunities to show off what they can do.

4 child-size tools Safety scissors, small-size gardening equipment, and housecleaning tools that really work let your child know that she's reached the stage where she can contribute in a meaningful way. Likewise, things like toy foods let your child enjoy imitative behavior, while stretching her imagination.

5 linking blocks Interlocking blocks encourage new kinds of building creations.

6 books Three year olds, who are particularly ego-centric, especially love personalized books, as well as books that support their personal interests.

7 art materials Paints, brushes, and easels or crayons and loads of paper continue to make great gifts. Add modeling clay, water paints, and other materials too.

8 costumes A variety of costumes encourages three-year-olds to act out their various moods and try out aspects of their emerging personalities.

9 videos Kids love videos because they let children indulge their love for watching the same thing over and over again. And, they allow parents to monitor the content of what their child is viewing more easily.

10 puppets These let your child act out the stories that are beginning to be written in his imagination.

11 dolls and stuffed animals At age three, these become objects of learning—collecting different kinds of bears or jungle animals, for example, teaches kids about nature—as well as continuing to offer comfort and the chance to develop nurturing skills.

12 toy musical instruments A variety of percussion instruments, such as drums, toy pianos, and xylophones, builds your child's auditory and rhythmic understanding.

13 cassette player Listening to favorite tunes and story tapes is a particularly fun activity at this stage.

14 visual toys Child-size binoculars and plastic magnifying glasses give your three-year-old a chance to get a close-up look at the world around her.

15 beginning board games Games designed for the youngest players, such as Candyland, I Spy, and Memory hone your child's thinking and social skills.

fabulous party favors for two- and three-year-olds

When choosing party favors, pay special attention to the age recommendations on the packaging and do not distribute items meant for older children to younger ones. Good choices include:

1 bubbles and wands Look for the nonspill variety.

2 play dough and a rolling pin Put them in a basket with a few cookie cutters.

3 chunky crayons and colored paper Roll up a few sheets and tie them with a ribbon.

4 colored pipe cleaners These fuzzy, pliable things provide hours of fun and creative play.

5 little books

6 animals Large plastic animals, animal nose masks, and animal crackers are sure to please.

7 plastic helmets A number of catalog merchants, such as Lillian Vernon, offer sets of six helmets designed as firefighter's hats, cowhand hats, and other designs.

8 personalized items Three-year-olds are beginning to recognize their own written names, so anything that bears each guest's name, such as a plastic cup or a picture frame, is perfect.

party activities for two-year-olds

Keep in mind that many twos are not yet ready for organized games. These activities can hold their attention for ten minutes or more:

1 chasing games Let the children run around chasing a big beach ball. Have enough beach balls so that no child is left without one. Other things to chase include soap bubbles and paper streamers.

2 follow-the-leader games Play noncompetitive versions of Simon says and follow the leader. Set up a safe obstacle course in which toddlers go in, under, around, and through various items.

3 storytime Read a rousing story, perhaps one that relates to the theme of the party, or create a puppet play, acting out a favorite story.

4 mural making Engage the kids in a common art project, such as painting or coloring a mural. Tape craft paper to a wall or the floor and encourage guests to fill it with their work. Or on a safe sidewalk in warm weather, provide chunky chalk or pails of water and large paintbrushes.

5 mazes Tape four to six large cartons together, cut out windows, and invite kids to weave their way through the maze.

more party activities for threes

I n addition to the above activities, which three-year-olds will still enjoy, try these for surefire fun:

1 musical chairs Adapt the game of musical chairs so that everyone gets a seat every time the music stops.

2 tossing games Let guests demonstrate their prowess at aiming and throwing. Using a large open carton or a laundry basket as the target, have kids take turns tossing in beanbags.

3 animal charades Have guests take turns acting out various animals while other guests guess what they are.

4 hunt and find Hide (in easy-to-find places) plastic eggs filled with treats. Instead of counting up who found the most, have all the guests place their finds in a central basket to be shared.

5 decorate food and favors Provide the ingredients; let kids decorate their own cupcakes, hats, and placemats.

6 have a parade Using toy instruments or home-made noisemakers, have kids parade around the room or the even neighborhood, accompanied by grown-up leaders. Or, instead of marching, decorate each child's tricycle with paper streamers and lead them on a riding parade.

7 sing-along If you can play the piano, guitar, or other instrument, get a kids' songbook and lead the guests in rousing renditions of familiar favorites.

party guest manners

toddlers are not known for exemplary social skills, but yours can learn to be a reasonably well behaved guest. To prepare your child for attending a friend's party:

1 explain expectations beforehand Clue your child in to what he can expect at the party. Note that the celebrant will be receiving presents, games will be played, food will be served, and that all guests get a special gift at the end of the party.

2 practice party manners Role-play ahead of time, letting your child practice giving a gift. Teach him to say "Happy birthday" and "Thank you for inviting me" and other polite gestures. Take turns blowing out birthday candles, reminding him that at the party, only the birthday child blows.

3 involve your child in choosing the gift
Choosing a gift for someone else can be a very difficult task for a toddler, especially when he's expected to give away something he may want for himself. One good way to help your child get into the spirit of sharing and choosing appropriate gifts is to purchase an item that your child already has and enjoys. Suggesting "Let's get Jake a dump truck just like yours so you can play with them together" helps your toddler experience the fun of giving without a sense of loss.

4 feed your toddler beforehand Avoid crankiness by making sure your toddler has a full stomach. Even if food will be served at the party, you can't be sure it will be something your child likes.

5 stick around Most toddlers are better able to handle the excitement of a party if you're close by.

when your child is the host

your toddler is used to being the center of your attention. At her own birthday party, she may be overwhelmed by the combination of having your attention diverted as well as being the focus of her guests' attention. To help your birthday child enjoy her day:

1 don't raise expectations too high Don't repeatedly tell your child how wonderful her party will be or say something like, "You can do anything you want because it's your special day." Instead, simply let her know that she and her friends can plan on having fun.

2 practice party manners Role-play ahead of time, letting your child practice receiving a gift. Teach her to meet and greet her guests and to say "Thank you" for her gifts and for coming to the party.

3 involve your child in the planning Within reason, let your toddler choose the party theme and favors. Let her distribute food and favors to her guests.

4 give her the same goodies as guests Make sure there are enough favors so that she gets one, too. If she wants to wear the same hat as guests instead of her special one, let her.

making memories

taking fabulous photos of your child

n o doubt, you're taking lots of pictures. To capture the best shots:

1 choose the right camera More important than lots of special features or costly lenses is simplicity of use. Have a point-and-shoot camera available so you don't miss great shots while fumbling with special settings.

2 keep your camera available Always having a camera on hand, even a disposable one that you keep in your diaper bag, helps ensure that you don't miss memorable moments.

3 use the right film Film speed determines how much light your pictures need to show contrast. A high-speed film captures light faster so you won't need as much light to get a properly exposed photo. Choose a speed of 400 or higher when shooting indoors or outdoors on a cloudy day. For shooting outdoors in sunshine, 100 or 200 is sufficient.

4 watch the background When focusing on your child, it's all too easy to ignore the backdrop until you see the developed pictures and something seems to be growing out of your child's head. Review the whole frame before snapping to avoid such shots.

5 go for close-ups The more your child's face fills the frame, the better. Just don't get so close that you crop off part of his head or blur the picture.

6 create your own frame Putting your child in a wide-brimmed hat or in front of a plain, bright-colored backdrop naturally frames him and creates a sharp image.

7 don't make him pose Now and again, don't let your child know he's being photographed, to avoid strained smiles, red-eye, and too many similar photos.

8 cover the angles Get down to eye level with your child rather than take pictures above him. Take some off-center shots to create more unusual compositions.

9 give your child another focus Take a picture while he's examining a new toy or tasting a new food for the first time to get a variety of natural, and sometimes amusing, expressions.

10 watch outdoor lighting Side lighting works best. When the sun is behind your child, you'll get a silhouette, and when the sun is in his face, you'll get both a scrunched-up expression and an overexposed picture.

preserving photos

n order to avoid becoming overwhelmed by piles of pictures:

1 edit Save only the best from each roll you develop. Send out the others with letters and save some in a box for your child to use for art projects.

2 use the right albums and frames Many albums and frames contain chemicals that cause the quality of the photographs to deteriorate over time. Place photos you want to save in nonacidic albums and frames, available at photo-supply shops.

3 make collages Assembling ordinary photos in a montage adds interest. You can group photos by theme, such as holiday celebrations, or by year, giving yourself an easy-to-view time capsule.

4 send personalized postcards Have your pictures developed in three-by-five-inch size in matte finish. Then paste them to the backs of instant postcard frames, available in many catalogs and photo shops.

making memorable movies

Camcorders capture your baby's routines and special events in fun ways. To make award-worthy films:

1 create a soundtrack Play Bach, Beatles, or your baby's favorite nursery songs in the background.

2 interview your subjects At a family gathering—particularly one that honors your baby—ask each guest to say something special to your child.

3 join the action Place the camcorder on a tripod and use the remote to tape yourself and your child as you read a favorite storybook and your child cuddles in your lap.

sharing your child's art

It would take a museum to display all of a toddler's artwork. To make sure that your child's work is seen without having to store everything:

1 use it as wrapping paper The recipient will love it, especially if the gift is for Grandma.

2 send it to relatives Roll it and place it in a paper tube, such as the cardboard tube from a roll of paper towels, and mail it with letters to appreciative relatives. Or scan and e-mail it.

3 hang it from an indoor clothesline In a hallway or entry foyer, string a line and use clothespins to hold the latest works for all to see.

4 take it along when you're on errands Let your child determine who along your daily route would like each work. Help him announce, "I made this and I want you to have it," and let him give a drawing to the grocery-store clerk, the mail carrier, or his pediatrician. He'll enjoy the accolades and may find his work displayed all over town.

5 organize a neighborhood art show Invite other parents to collect and display their children's artwork in the playground or other public place.

upsets **and** changes

coping with moving

toddlers thrive on routine, so moving can be a traumatic experience. To lessen the upset:

1 plan for when there aren't other big changes
If at all possible, don't move in the weeks surrounding the birth of a sibling, for instance. Two such enormous changes are difficult for your toddler to handle all at once.

2 introduce your child's new home in advance
Again, if possible, take your child on one or more tours of the new house before moving in.

3 make a special moving book Have your child draw pictures and take some photos of both the new and the old house. Let her dictate captions for each image.

4 read storybooks about moving Some toddler-appropriate titles include *A Tale of Two Houses* by Melody Carlson (Zondervan Publishing), *Good-bye, House* by Robin Ballard (Greenwillow), *Little Monster's Moving Day* by Mercer Mayer (Cartwheel), and *The Berenstain Bears' Moving Day* by Jan and Stan Berenstain (Random House).

5 disassemble your child's room last As you prepare to move, don't pack up your child's room until last. Keep special items, such as her bedtime books and toys, with you rather than putting them on the moving van.

6 set up your child's room first At the new house, prepare your child's room first so that she can feel at home right away.

7 arrange an activity for your child If possible, during part of the move have a person your child knows well accompany you on moving day to keep your child safely and happily out of the way of the movers. Don't, however, keep your older toddler completely out of the picture since seeing her things go into the new house helps her understand what is happening.

8 help make the unfamiliar seem familiar On moving day, let your child enjoy her favorite lunch on her favorite plate. Read familiar bedtime stories.

9 show enthusiasm for the move Moving can be traumatic for you, too, but it's best not to indulge in emotional displays in front of your toddler. Emphasize the positive.

handling separation and divorce

I f you and your spouse are separating or divorcing, you can help your toddler understand and withstand the events in these ways:

1 reassure your child of your love Tell your child explicitly that both parents continue to love him even if you do not both live with him.

2 explain that the separation is not his fault Egocentric toddlers need to understand that their actions have nothing whatsoever to do with you and your spouse's decision.

3 maintain contact Never let your own relationship with your ex interfere with his or her relationship with your child. In almost all circumstances, your child is better off maintaining and continuing to build a relationship with his other parent. Be as flexible as possible in arranging custody and visitation.

4 never badmouth the other parent Keep any negative opinions to yourself. Note similarities between your child and your ex only in positive ways, saying for instance, "You have beautiful brown eyes, just like your dad."

5 put your child first If at all possible, consider arrangements that allow your child to stay in one place while parents take turns with him rather than having your child move around, at least at first.

coping with a hospital stay

for both parents and kids, the prospect of a hospital stay can be overwhelming. To help everyone deal with it:

1 remain calm Appearing fearful only adds to your child's confusion and upset. When you are with your child, do your best to control your emotions.

2 tour the hospital beforehand If possible, show your older toddler the room where he will sleep and the hospital playroom. If he's going to need a general anesthesia, let him see and touch the mask beforehand, if your child will be receiving anesthesia by this method. Don't overload him with information, however. Find out where you can sleep if you'll be staying with your child, and what provisions, in general, the hospital makes for parents.

3 read appropriate books and view videos For toddlers, those about hospitals include *A Visit to the Sesame Street Hospital* by Deborah Hautzig and Dan Elliot (Random House), *Going to the Hospital* by Anne Civardi and Stephen Cartwright (Educational Development Corporation), and *Rita Goes to the Hospital* by Martine Davison (Random House).

4 meet with the child-life specialist Many hospital facilities have a staff person whose specialty is helping families during a medical crisis. Be sure to avail yourself of this service.

5 don't ask your child to be brave It's perfectly normal for a child to cry during procedures and at various points throughout a hospital stay. While you need to help your child cooperate with medical procedures, assure him that it's okay to cry while you comfort him.

6 insist on appropriate pain medication Find out what medications are suitable for your child and see that they are used to block pain when appropriate.

7 don't lie If a procedure will hurt, don't say it won't in order to secure your child's cooperation. Instead say, "This may hurt a bit, but I'm going to hold you and do my best to make you feel better soon."

8 have comforting items from home on hand If the hospital allows it, bring your child's own pajamas and favorite blanket as well as a stuffed animal or doll that can comfort him.

9 take care of yourself Arrange for some respite to keep your own strength up.

helping your child understand illness and death

Your child's closeness to a person is the primary factor in how much she needs to know about an illness or death. Your toddler is unlikely to be affected by the illness or death of a person she's had little contact with, though she will, of course, be affected by your behavior. To help your child:

1 monitor your own reactions You can't be expected to refrain from showing any emotion when you're coping with the illness or death of a loved one. However, in the presence of your toddler, do your best to remain in control.

2 don't use euphemisms Never say that a person who has died "went to sleep," which can make your child fearful of sleeping.

3 be careful in discussing illness If you are discussing a serious illness in front of your child, be careful to differentiate types of illnesses. For instance, you might note that "Grandma is very, very sick. She might not get better. But most people *do* get better. *You* always get better when you get sick."

4 reassure your child When your child sees that you're upset, reassure her that she did not cause your sad feelings and assure her that she is safe.

5 limit your toddler's exposure There's nothing for a toddler to gain from attending a funeral. Let her attend one only if there's ample opportunity for her to be taken outside if she needs to run around.

6 have ongoing discussions about the life cycle

Even a three-year-old can understand that people and other living things go through cycles of birth, growth, and death. Point out springtime buds and autumn's falling leaves.

7 read age-appropriate books

Reading books about illness or death can help you explain these concepts to your child. Some suggestions are *What's Heaven?* by Maria Shriver (Golden Books), *Jinka Jinka Jelly Bean* by Molly Dingles (Dingles & Company), *When Dinosaurs Die: A Guide to Understanding Death* by Marc Tolon Brown (Little Brown), *The Tenth Good Thing About Barney* by Judith Viorst (Aladdin), and *The Fall of Freddie the Leaf* by Leo Buscaglia (Holt Rinehart & Winston).

relationships

siblings and only children

when baby makes four: welcoming a new sibling

Your toddler's reaction to the birth of a sibling can range from excitement and pride to feelings of abandonment and betrayal—sometimes all in the course of a single day. Moving from the uncontested center of his universe to the role of big kid can certainly be traumatic. To ease the transition:

1 work toward having sufficient one-on-one time At the moment that you introduce the new sibling to your toddler, have someone else hold the baby so that you can invite your toddler into your arms for the introduction. Over the next few weeks, while your toddler is adjusting, make a point of maintaining as much cuddle time as he's used to, and maybe even some more. Plan special time with your toddler while the baby sleeps or when possible, arrange for someone else to watch the baby while you play with your big kid.

2 appeal to his sense of pride Make a big deal once in a while about his new role as big brother. Note that there are so many things that he can do that his baby sister or brother cannot do, and let him demonstrate such talents, like hopping or singing.

3 remind him of his babyhood Share pictures with him of his own infancy. Tell him the story of the day he was born.

4 accept some regression Don't be surprised—or punitive—if your trained toddler suddenly needs a diaper or if he insists on crawling. Don't make a big deal about "accidents." Respond to babyish behavior by acknowledging that he's not really a baby anymore and, if necessary, by setting limits on these actions. For example, if your child wants a bottle, say, "I bet you like pretending you're a baby."

5 don't initiate other big changes now Make any
necessary changes at least a month before or after the
baby's arrival—starting your child in nursery school,
moving to a new house, moving him from his crib to
a toddler bed, or weaning him from breast or bottle.

6 don't push their relationship But don't interfere
either. Don't insist that your toddler act thrilled about
the baby. Nor should you be overly critical when he
gets close to your newborn. If your toddler insists
that you take the new baby back, don't react harshly.
Acknowledge his feelings and say something like, "I
know you're not always happy to have a new baby in
the house." Then remind him that the baby is part of
the family. When your toddler shows curiosity about his
new sibling, follow his lead and let him have a close-up
look. Guide his hand gently over the baby's arm, saying
something like, "She likes it when you touch her gently."

making multiples feel unique

Whether you're raising identical twins or fraternal
quads, you want to be sure that each of your children
thrives as an individual as well as being a proud member of
her own special group. To help each of your children develop
her special talents:

1 avoid sound-alike names Names that rhyme or
begin with the same letter set your children up for a
lifetime of being seen as part of a group. Each child
deserves a name all her own. If your children do have
too-similar names, consider letting one or more go
by different-sounding middle names or nicknames.

2 limit dress-alike outfits Your twins' (or quints')
mirror images are best kept in the mirror. From the
time they are able to recognize their own clothing,
help them choose outfits that reflect their own tastes.

3 find one-on-one time with each Take turns with your spouse and other family members and sitters to spend time alone with each child. If this doesn't happen naturally in the course of each week, schedule special times alone with each child and do your best to keep your dates.

4 arrange playdates with other children When your child comes with a built-in peer, it's easy not to look elsewhere for playmates, but introducing other children to yours helps them find pleasure in a wider range of companionship. Also, multiples are notorious for creating their own private language, largely because they spend so much time playing together as they are developing. Introducing others to their circle helps keep their language skills growing at the pace they would if they were singletons.

5 provide separate spaces While you may not be able to provide each child with her own room, be sure that each has a special place for her things. For instance, rather than putting all of the kids' tee shirts in one drawer and all of the pants in another, have separate drawers for each child's clothes.

6 expect toddlers to act like toddlers Don't expect that just because your children shared a womb that they want to share everything else. Just like children born singly, your toddlers will need to learn the fine art of sharing in a deliberate way.

7 honor individual tastes Recognize that your children, even if identical in appearance, may have disparate tastes. As much as possible, respect those differences. While it isn't necessary to make each child her favorite lunch each day, be accommodating when you can be.

8 speak to them separately Don't call them "the twins." Use their individual names. Don't ask, "What would you"—referring to more than one—"like to eat?" Limit choices and ask, "Hannah, would you like tuna salad or a cheese sandwich? Jill, which one would you prefer?"

Sibling squabbles are a fact of life in any home with more than one child. So, while you can't expect to eliminate all disagreements, there are some things you can do to minimize sibling battles, including:

1 focus on each child's individual needs It's impossible to treat each child equally, so don't even try. Besides, even if you did manage to dish out exact-same-size portions to two kids, each would swear that the other got more. So when your three-year-old complains that you're spending too much time carrying his baby sister, say, "Your baby sister needs me to carry her. You need me to read you stories." Or when your two-year-old cries that he wants to play with his big sister's bicycle, say, "Her bike fits her and your bike fits you."

2 give each child special time with you At least once a week, plan a special date with each child. Let each one know that everyone's special time is sacred. During an older child's special time, make sure your toddler is engaged in an activity with another caring adult or give your older child his special time while your toddler naps.

3 don't compare kids It's tempting to tell your whining four-year-old to speak nicely like his three-year-old sibling or vice versa. Far better, however, is to focus on the whiner and say, "I can't listen while you whine. Use your good voice." Leave any mention of his sibling out of the discussion.

4 be aware of favoritism It's natural to feel closer to one child than another now and then due to differences in temperament, but it's important to avoid being obvious in treating children differently.

5 respect each child's space Don't let your toddler destroy a drawing that your five-year-old slaved over. Help your older child protect his stuff while protecting the younger one from the dangers of toys meant for older kids.

6 catch them being kind to one another

Commenting favorably when they do get along is far more effective in engendering good mutual feeling than responding only to squabbles. Make a point of saying, "I like seeing you play so well together" when they do, even if only for a moment.

7 don't always assume the older child is at fault

A four- or even a ten-year-old can't be expected to be forever patient with a toddler. Even a two-year-old can learn to respect his older sibling's space and belongings.

8 don't expect older siblings to baby-sit

Even children who are old enough to baby-sit for the neighbors shouldn't be expected to be in-house baby-sitters. While a young teen can certainly watch your younger child for a moment now and then, it's vital that he be allowed to enjoy age-appropriate activities outside the family.

9 don't interfere too much

As long as no one's being physically or emotionally hurt, direct your children to work out their own problems as much as possible.

10 never allow physical or verbal abuse

While angry feelings are almost inevitable, don't allow one child to physically or emotionally harm another. React swiftly and firmly to any act of violence among siblings.

only doesn't have to be lonely

just as kids from families with more than one child need special time with their parents, singletons miss certain benefits that children with siblings enjoy. To compensate for a lack of siblings:

1 plan peer-group activities Enroll your child in playgroups and have frequent playdates so that she can learn the give-and-take of relationships.

2 help your child make friends of various ages Give your child the opportunity to learn from kids a year or two older and to teach and nurture younger children.

3 develop strong relationships with relatives Help your child develop relationships with extended family, especially close-in-age cousins, who share a history.

4 engage in group activities When your child reaches school age, encourage her to join organized groups that foster teamwork. Have sleepovers so your child can learn to accommodate others' needs, like sleeping with the light on if that's what a visiting friend requires.

5 don't overindulge Without the pressure of providing for more than one child it can be tempting to try to give your child more material possessions than she needs. Make sure that your child does not stand out among her peers as being the first to get every new thing on the market.

6 focus on how your child reacts to fights Your child may need instruction in how to keep relationships with friends going in spite of spats, something siblings learn early on.

7 extend your own social life Invite another family with kids to dinner. Go as far as to plan a vacation with another family, so that your child gets to experience the ups and downs of a normal day with other kids.

spouses

great gifts for new moms

1 time at a spa Whether it's a day of massages or a 30-minute facial, a pampering treatment can restore a new mom's body and soul.

2 a beauty treatment A gift certificate to a salon for a manicure or pedicure is sure to lift mom's mood.

3 comfy, attractive clothes For the time between maternity clothing and the pre-pregnancy wardrobe, anything soft and pretty (and that doesn't show spit-up stains) is welcome.

4 self-care products Bath beads and thick Turkish towels, aromatherapy oils and candles—these can work wonders in the limited time available while baby naps.

5 prepared foods In addition to the casseroles and family dinners that can save mom work, toss in a few extravagant items.

6 time Offer an afternoon or even just an hour in which a new parent can relax, run an errand, or visit friends.

7 company and help Caring for an infant can be isolating, especially in harsh weather when the baby can't be taken out, so offer to come by and help out.

8 tickets to a show and baby-sitting A night out can give new parents a wonderful way to get reacquainted without the baby in tow.

great gifts for new dads

though dad may not be recovering from the birth in quite the same way as his mate, his new role requires honoring, too. Consider:

1 film, batteries, and prepaid film developing
There's never enough film around for a new dad, batteries go dead when baby is doing something adorable, and the cost of film developing can eat into junior's college fund.

2 a dad-designed diaper bag Most dads (and many moms) would prefer not to carry a pink bag decorated with bunnies. Look for something in dark canvas.

3 stroller handle extenders Tall dads may be uncomfortable pushing a stroller that's just the right height for their mates. Stroller handle extenders, available at most baby supply stores, keep dads from getting backaches.

4 matching gear Get baseball caps for baby and dad that feature dad's favorite team.

5 a book on child care He'll enjoy becoming an expert.

6 a baby carrier Once the baby gets a bit bigger, dad will have an easier time carrying the baby around than mom will.

sharing the caring with your spouse

the arrival of a child shifts parents' attention from each other to the new baby in their midst. Inevitably, primarily during the newborn stage, one parent (usually mom, especially if she is breast-feeding) has most of the responsibility for child care. Over time, both parents might want to work toward a more equitable arrangement. Here's how:

1 trust that both parents can care for the baby

Many new moms fear that their baby's dad lacks the instinct to care for a newborn properly. Likewise, many new dads fear doing something wrong. While moms and dads may do things differently, there's rarely a right and a wrong way of caring for a newborn, and common sense and a few nonjudgmental instructions are all that's necessary. If you're a new mom and the primary caregiver, trust your partner to care for your baby. Leave him in charge, while you take a walk or simply relax. Other than breast-feeding, there's nothing he can't do. If you're a new dad, don't feel that your lack of experience excludes you from your important role. If you're unsure of what to do, ask for advice or read up on baby care, but don't consider yourself helpless. Developing a relationship with your child can't wait until he's older.

2 equity doesn't mean splitting every task 50-50

One partner may stay at home to care for your child and your home while the other is the breadwinner. One may have to work 12-hour days while the other is able to be home at dinner. Consider each person's contribution to the family rather than insist on an equal split when it comes to child care. Talk about any imbalances that you feel are keeping either of you from maintaining your relationship or from forming a close relationship with your child. Then work together to resolve them.

3 don't take on rigid roles with your child
Your child benefits in knowing that either parent can feed, bathe, and clothe him, that either parent can be counted on to soothe a hurt or correct a misbehavior.

4 get outside help
If housework overwhelms either of you, consider hiring help. Spending that money may

mean that you'll be enjoying an afternoon at the playground rather than at the movies, but it may keep you in a calmer frame of mind and ensure that your family is better able to enjoy the time together.

5 schedule individual time with your child For your child's sake, as well as to give each other a break, plan a time at least once a week when one parent is fully engaged with your child, while the other takes a break.

making your mate feel competent

few parents have any instinctual sense of how to care for a newborn. Both moms and dads often feel ill-at-ease when faced with a squirming infant. If you are the primary caregiver, you can help your mate feel competent in handling your baby by encouraging him to:

1 assume most responsibility for specific tasks In the long run, your spouse will feel at ease in all aspects of child care. But during the newborn phase, it might help to turn over all the responsibility for one or more aspects of child care. For instance, your spouse can take care of all the diaper changes and or middle-of-the-night bottles, gaining competence and confidence in one area that will spread to others.

2 go out alone with the baby Taking the baby for a walk and socializing with other parents deepens your spouse's sense of involvement and connection with your newborn.

3 spend time alone at home with the baby It's equally important for your spouse to spend time alone at home caring for the baby so that he learns he can handle the situation without relying on you.

4 get to know others in the baby-care team Take turns with your spouse bringing your child for his scheduled doctor visits. Mom and dad both can arrange for child care and playdates.

a little romance

passion made you parents. Don't let parenthood get in the way of keeping your love alive.

1 keep the focus on each other As remarkable as your new baby is, don't lose sight of your partner. Make a point of complimenting each other's appearance. Keep up with each other's work and interests.

2 make time away from your baby At least once a month, more if possible, make a date with your spouse to get out of the house and do something fun together.

3 don't feel guilty Realize that time spent together nurturing your relationship is the best gift you can give to your child.

4 talk Being parents can change the way you view each other. Talk about your new feelings and expectations. Listen to each other.

5 be romantic at home There's no law against having a candlelight dinner with a child in a bouncy seat nearby. Seeing her parents being affectionate makes your child feel part of something very special. And making everyday occasions romantic helps you realize that parenthood hasn't altered your fundamental feelings toward your partner.

extended family

bonding with grandparents

a strong relationship with grandparents provides children with a sense of history and belonging.

1 be open-minded Child-rearing philosophies have changed over the generations, but not all of grandma or granddad's ideas are outdated. Share your thoughts on various issues and listen to your parents' and in-laws' ideas. Realize that all of you have your child's best interests at heart.

2 keep grandparents posted Schedule regular visits with nearby grandparents. Have frequent mail and phone communication with faraway grandparents, and send photos and videos so that they can experience the exciting progress your child is making every day.

3 help your child get to know them Regular contact allows your child and his grandparents to form a close bond. If your parents or in-laws do not live nearby, keep current photos of them prominently displayed.

4 encourage one-on-one communication After the infant stage, let your child talk with them on the phone. Suggest that he send his latest artwork to them.

5 use technology Exchange e-mail with scanned photos. Make a video of your child saying "Hi" to his grandparents and showing off his latest skill. Ask grandparents to videotape themselves reading one of your child's favorite books aloud.

handling grandparents' advice on child rearing

I t's a rare grandparent who can resist sharing his or her opinion on how you're raising your child. To handle unasked-for advice:

1 establish your credentials Rather than simply defending your ideas, share books and articles that support your way of thinking. By backing up your practices with facts, you can, for instance, be firm in matters of health and safety without appearing willful.

2 be flexible In less serious matters, don't overreact if your child's grandparents do things somewhat differently from the way you would do them.

3 listen Part of your dialogue with your child's grandparents includes listening to their ideas.

4 be tactful Instead of responding to advice with a statement such as "That's not how I want to do it," respond with a less hostile "I'll think about that."

child-care providers

child-care options

Your needs, your child's needs, convenience, and cost are the factors you'll be considering when choosing child care. Here's a primer about your options and your responsibilities regarding each type of care:

1 in-home care A sitter comes to your home and may either live in or commute. Your primary concern is choosing a person you can trust to provide physical and emotional care for your child. It's essential to check the sitter's references, even if you have used an agency to do your preliminary screening, and to monitor the arrangement regularly. Also, be aware that you are responsible for filing taxes and providing other compensation, such as paid sick leave and vacation.

2 family day care In this arrangement, your child is cared for in another's home along with a number of other children of varying ages. As with in-home care, you need to check references carefully. While a state license is not a guarantee that the care provider meets your needs, it does denote that she has met minimal state requirements for health and safety.

3 child-care centers Centers range from small private ones to large corporate-based or franchise operations. Choose only a licensed center and talk to parents whose children attend the center.

advantages and drawbacks of:

in-home care

The benefits of in-home care include:

1 convenience An in-home sitter allows you to leave your child sleeping when you head off to an early-morning meeting as well as to arrive home later—provided, of course, that you have made prior arrangements with your sitter. Your sitter will also be able to take care of a mildly ill child.

2 health Especially for babies under six months of age, the lack of exposure to other kids' germs is a real plus.

3 relationships You, your child, and your sitter have an opportunity to develop a long-term, mutually satisfying relationship.

family day care

The benefits of a family day-care setting include:

1 more flexibility than most child-care centers An individual caregiver is more apt to support your need for flexible hours than a larger center.

2 family setting Your child is exposed to kids his own age, younger, and older, getting a chance to learn and interact with a variety of children.

3 lower cost Family centers tend to be less costly than either in-home care or large centers.

Disadvantages include:

1 higher cost In most cases, one-on-one care is substantially more expensive than group care.

2 lack of backup If your sitter is sick or suddenly quits, you'll have to find a replacement.

3 lack of oversight Your sitter is not monitored during the time she spends alone with your child.

4 lack of learning opportunities for your child Solitary care may not offer the social interaction that quality group care does.

Disadvantages include:

1 exposure to other kids' germs

2 lack of backup If your sitter is sick or suddenly decides to quit the business, you'll have to find a replacement.

3 lack of oversight Your sitter is not monitored during the time she spends with the children in her care, although other parents are available for their opinions.

advantages and drawbacks of:

child-care centers

The benefits of a child-care center include:

1 the likelihood of trained personnel Centers are more likely to have trained early-childhood professionals on staff.

2 social interactions Your child gets to know other kids his own age and parents are able to meet others with same- or similar-aged children.

3 continuity Centers provide the most stability and are not likely to shut down if an individual teacher leaves.

4 oversight A multilayered operation provides oversight by center directors, other teachers, and a variety of parents.

Disadvantages include:

1 exposure to other kids' germs

2 inflexible policies Rules often prohibit you from bringing in a mildly ill child. You'll need backup care for days your child is under the weather.

3 personnel turnover A high rate of turnover, which is a problem at some centers, lessens the chance that your child will form a close attachment with his caregiver.

W hether you're choosing a child-care center for daily care or a baby-sitter for a single evening:

1 seek recommendations Begin your search by asking other parents for recommendations of individuals and/or agencies.

2 always check references Ask for the phone numbers of others for whom the sitter has worked and talk to the parents. Ask for any reasons why they would or would not hire this person again.

3 allow time to see the sitter with your child
Have the sitter come over before you plan to leave your child with her so you can see how they interact.

4 trust your gut feelings If something doesn't feel right to you, don't hire a particular sitter. It's far better to err on the side of caution.

parents ALERT!

child-to-caregiver ratios Be sure that the child-care setting you choose has a high ratio of staff to children. Ideally, the center should have no more than three infants to one staff member, four one-year-olds to one staff member, six two-year-olds to one staff member, and eight three-year-olds to one staff member.

questions to ask your baby-sitter

I f your choose an in-home sitter to care for your child, be sure to ask:

1 what child-care experiences have you had?
Ask the sitter to recall the best and the worst experiences. The details can be telling.

2 what is your relationship with the last family for whom you baby-sat?

3 how do you handle discipline? Be specific. Ask her what she would do if your baby cried for an hour. What if your toddler was inattentive or defiant? What would she do if your child broke a favorite item of hers or ruined an outfit, intentionally or not?

4 how do you feel about TV watching? Does she plan to watch TV while your child naps? Does she offer TV or video viewing as a regular daily activity?

5 do you agree with my rules for my child? If not, can she abide by them anyway?

6 do you mingle with other sitters and parents? How comfortable is she with other caregivers? Does she enjoy taking a child out to meet others?

7 what do you know about nutrition? What does she consider good meals and snacks for your toddler?

8 what would you do in an emergency? How would she react if your child suddenly became ill, was injured, or if there was a fire?

9 how do you envision spending your day? Will she be providing ample stimulation and planning age-appropriate activities and outings?

dealing with your nanny

hiring a nanny may be your first experience as an employer. Here's how to handle your position in a way that benefits you, your child, and your sitter:

1 realize that the sitter has a life of her own You may think of her as a part of your family, but she has got her own life and perhaps her own children. Invite her to join family activities that are not part of her job, but don't feel rejected if she chooses not to come.

2 be mindful of your agreement Don't expect your sitter to accept additional hours or responsibilities without additional pay or to alter her plans at the last minute to meet your schedule. Plan ahead and check any changes with her. Likewise, pay her on time and in full, including any earned overtime.

3 respect cultural differences Unless a cultural difference or a difference in beliefs and attitudes affects your child's well-being, realize that exposure to the ideas of others can be a good thing for your child.

4 be respectful Speak to your sitter the same way you'd speak to another adult, rather than assume a superior position. Don't correct her in front of your child. If an issue needs to be discussed, set aside time to talk with her privately and be sure to listen as well as talk.

evaluating health and safety standards

here's what to look for when judging the safety and cleanliness of any group-care setting:

1 running water, soap, and paper towels These supplies should be readily available.

2 toys are cleaned regularly Baby toys should be washed daily and disinfected at least twice a week. All play equipment is in good repair and is age-appropriate.

3 safety is built in Windows, stairways, and doors are safely designed and off-limits to your child.

4 diapering areas are away from play Eating areas should be disinfected between uses too.

5 bathrooms and kitchens are disinfected daily Trash is kept out of children's reach and removed daily.

6 food is stored safely Perishable food, including lunches and snacks from home, are stored in the refrigerator. Other foods are kept in containers at least six inches off the floor.

7 electrical outlets are covered Protective plugs should cover all electrical outlets not in use.

8 unsafe materials are locked away Potentially dangerous materials, including medicines and cleaning supplies, are stored in their original containers and in locked cabinets.

9 smoke detectors and fire extinguishers These should be easily accessible to the staff.

10 emergency evacuation plan All staff members should be trained to act in an emergency, and there should be a plan in effect.

11 emergency-certified staff At least one staff person should be certified for emergency pediatric first aid and CPR.

specific things to look for in a child-care center

When visiting child-care centers, consider the following, in addition to the items listed on pages 149–151, for reviewing nursery schools:

1 the overall appearance of the center Is it well lit, clean, and generally cheery? Are furnishings, including toilets, child-sized?

2 attention to health and safety issues Does the center meet or exceed the standards outlined in Evaluating Health and Safety Standards (above)?

3 qualified staff Head teachers and the center's director should have training in early-childhood education and development. All staff members who work with children should demonstrate a suitable temperament.

4 range of activities There should be a mix of group and individual activities as well as indoor and outdoor play areas.

5 educational policy Does the center provide appropriate formal learning in addition to child-care services?

great websites

need a roadmap to the best sites on the web? Here are some landmark destinations that can give you up-to-date information on just about any aspect of raising your toddler. (For the most current sites, search AskJeeves.com for "parent information.")

- **BabyCenter.com** (for prenatal through preschool information)

- **cpsc.gov** (The U.S. Consumer Product Safety Commission to find out about product recalls or to report any problems with products); or call 800-638-2772; 800-638-8270 for the hearing impaired

- **ctw.org** (CTW family workshop, developed by Children's Television Workshop/Sesame Street)

- **drkoop.com** (developed by former U.S. Surgeon General, focuses on health issues)

- **eSCORE.com** (developed by Kaplan Education services)

- **familyeducation.com** (information on preschool through high school education)

- **KidsHealth.org** (for up-to-date health information)

- **naeyc.org** (site of the National Association for the Education of Young Children)

- **nickjr.com** (developed by Nickelodeon)

- **NPIN.org** (the National Parent Information Network, developed by the U.S. Department of Education); they also have phone help line at 800-583-4135

- **ParenthoodWeb.com** (a great general-interest site)

- **Parents.com** (featuring articles from *Child*, *Family Circle*, *Fitness*, *McCall's*, and *Parents* magazines)

- **ParentsPlace.com** (a great general-interest site and a service of iVillage.com)

- **Parentsoup.com** (a service of iVillage.com)

C omplete this list and keep it posted near your phone for emergencies.

EMERGENCY: 911

If your area is not served by the 911 system, the local emergency numbers are:

fire

ambulance

police

Poison Control Center: POI-SONS (764-7667)

If your area is not served by this number, the local poison-control number is:

(To find the poison control center nearest you, go to www.aapcc.org.)

your name

your address

your home phone #

(The above is essential for the baby-sitter, who may forget during an emergency.)

your work phone #

your spouse's work phone #

your cell phone #

your spouse's cell phone #

a neighbor's name and phone #

a relative's name and phone number #